T0266071

POCKET **ROUGH GUIDE**
TOKYO

written and researched by
MARTIN ZATKO

CONTENTS

TOKYO

With its sushi and sumo, geisha and gardens, neon and noodles, it may seem that Tokyo is in danger of collapsing under the weight of its own stereotypes. Yet ticking off a bunch of travel clichés is rarely this much fun, and as you might expect of the planet's largest metropolis, there's also enough nuance here to keep you entertained for a lifetime. Ordered yet bewildering, Japan's pulsating capital will lead you a merry dance: this is Asia at its weirdest, straightest, prettiest, sleaziest and coolest, all at the same time.

Imperial Palace

Ginza shopping district

Caught up in an untidy web of overhead cables, plagued by seemingly incessant noise, the concrete and steel conurbation may seem the stereotypical urban nightmare. Yet step back from the frenetic main roads and chances are you'll find yourself in tranquil backstreets, where dinky **wooden houses** are fronted by neatly clipped bonsai trees; wander beyond the high-tech emporia, and you'll discover charming fragments of the old city such as **temples** and **shrines** wreathed in wisps of smoking incense.

One way to ease yourself into the city is by taking a relatively crowd-free turn around the **Imperial Palace** – the inviolate home of the emperor and a tangible link to the past. From here it's a quick hop to glitzy **Ginza**, while the Edo-era spirit of the city lingers on in Tokyo's evocative northeast quarter; here, **Asakusa**'s primary focus is the major Buddhist temple of **Sensō-ji**, surrounded by a plethora of traditional craft shops, while the leafy precincts of **Ueno Park** contain several major museums. Also nearby is the weird, wired and wonderful **Akihabara** area, famous worldwide for its electronics stores, and recently

What's new

Tokyo was awarded the Summer Games in 2013, and spent years preparing for its hosting of the event in 2020; the main addition was the New National Stadium, designed by Pritzker Prize-winning architect Kengo Kuma. Another major change came down Tokyo Bay way, where Tsukiji's famous fish market was moved to modern new facilities in Toyosu. Lastly, an imperial succession in 2019 moved all of Japan into a new era, named "Reiwa".

INTRODUCTION

When to visit

One of the best times to visit is in the spring, from April to early May, when flurries of falling cherry blossom give the city a soft pink hue and temperatures are pleasant. October and November are also good for the fireburst of **autumn** leaves in Tokyo's parks and gardens. Avoid the steamy height of **summer** (late July to early Sept); from January through to March temperatures can dip to freezing, but the crisp blue **winter** skies are rarely disturbed by rain or snow showers. Carrying an umbrella is a good idea the rainy season in June and July, and in September, when typhoons occasionally strike the coast.

rebooted as the focus of Tokyo's dynamic manga and anime scene.

South of Ginza, and linked to the mainland by the impressive Rainbow Bridge, is **Odaiba**, a futuristic man-made island; heading west instead will bring you to nightlife-heavy **Roppongi**, now also something of an art haven. Fashionistas should head towards on-trend **Shibuya** and **Harajuku**, and the super-chic, boutique-lined boulevards of **Aoyama**. Also on the west side of

the city lies **Shinjuku**, bursting with towering skyscrapers, endless amounts of neon, TV screens several storeys tall, and arguably the world's most complicated railway station.

Tokyo is, quite literally, a "city of cities", with each of its mega-conurbations boasting a different character to the last, and all lassoed together by the above-ground Yamanote rail line – whichever Tokyo you desire is ready and waiting for your visit.

Old Imperial Bar

Where to...

Eat

Culinary quality is high across the board in Tokyo, and the best places to eat are spread quite liberally around the city, but there are distinctive elements to each neighbourhood. Head to Shinjuku, Ebisu or Ginza to eat at a yokochō, which are market-style areas packed with dozens of minuscule eateries. Then there's the new fish market in Toyosu – quite simply one of the world's best places for sushi – or dinner cruises on one of the lantern-strung yakatabune boats in Tokyo Bay. Ginza is best for tea, while Shibuya has the best array of cafés; however, you can head almost anywhere for great noodles, since there are thousands of noodle bars across the city.
OUR FAVOURITES: Omoide Yokochō (see page 101), Sushi-bun (see page 63), Cha Ginza (see page 37), Funasei (see page 63), Udon Shin (see page 101).

Drink

You won't go thirsty in Tokyo, from the fancy bars around Ginza and the Imperial Palace to the more rustic Hoppy-purveyors of Asakusa. Roppongi is famed for its nightlife (as well as for Japanese eager to meet foreigners), while Nakameguro has a more hipsterfied scene. However, you're bound to have at least one night out in Tokyo's two biggies – youthful Shibuya, home to more bars than you can count; and slightly seedy Shinjuku, likewise busy from nighttime into the early morning (even on weekdays), and home to the city's biggest LGBTQ scene.
OUR FAVOURITES: Old Imperial Bar (see page 31), Baja (see page 77), Commune (see page 90), The Lockup (see page 103).

Shop

Stacked with department stores and brand shops, Ginza is still regarded as Tokyo's traditional shopping centre, but funkier Shibuya and Harajuku are probably the most enjoyable places to shop. Even if you don't want to buy, the passing fashion parade doesn't get much better. Asakusa is home to a plethora of small, traditional crafts shops, while Akihabara has long been known as "electric town" thanks to its myriad high-tech emporia, and is also now the go-to location for manga and anime goods. Chic Daikanyama has an appealing village atmosphere and is a good place to check out up-and-coming Japanese designers.
OUR FAVOURITES: Jūsan-ya (see page 50), Dover Street Market (see page 36), Toraya (see page 69), The Cover Nippon (see page 69).

Go out

The Tokyo clubbing scene took a turn for the better in 2016, when a *Footloose*-like law forbidding dancing was finally repealed; the law had banned dancing in licensed premises after midnight, though in practice it was largely ignored, so not all that much has changed, especially in the main clubbing regions, **Roppongi** and **Shibuya**. Local **DJs** to look out for are Satoshi Tomiie, a house legend since the early '90s; Ken Ishii, well known for his techno sets; EDM attitude-monger Mitomi Tokoto; and quirky dubstep star Ajapai.
OUR FAVOURITES: Muse (see page 71), Bonobo (see page 89), Harlem (see page 91), Womb (see page 91).

Tokyo at a glance

Ikebukuro and the north p.104.
Working-class Ikebukuro has a few gems up its sleeve, particularly the gorgeous ornamental gardens just to its east.

Ueno and around p.46.
Perhaps the city's best sightseeing zone, so long as the weather plays ball, with an array of great sights strung around a beautiful lake.

Shinjuku and the west p.92.
A mass of neon-pulsing high-rise, Shinjuku is essentially a city in itself, and one of Tokyo's most characterful areas.

Harajuku and Shibuya p.78.
Harajuku is the Tokyo many people imagine – almost like a fashion show for the weird and wonderful – while the mega-neighbourhood of Shibuya exudes more energy than most countries do.

Ebisu and the south p.72.
A spread-out clutch of neighbourhoods just south of central Tokyo, each with their own distinctive atmosphere.

Akasaka and Roppongi p.64.
Famed for nightlife and higher-end dining, these areas are also the city's most appealing for art buffs.

SUGAMO · Rikugi-en · NISHI-IKEBUKURO · HIGASHI-IKEBUKURO · MEJIRODAI · Chinzan-sō · KAGURAZAKA · KOREATOWN · NISHI-SHINJUKU · KABUKICHŌ · GOLDEN GAI · HIGASHI-SHINJUKU · SHINJUKU-NICHŌME · Shinjuku Gyoen · Meiji-jingū · Inner Garden · Jingū Naien · Yoyogi-kōen · HARAJUKU · JINGŪMAE · AOYAMA · SHIBUYA · DŌGENZAKA · DAIKANYAMA · HIRO-O · EBISU · Meiji-jingū Outer Garden · AKASAKA · MINATO-KU · Hinokichō-kōen · TOKYO MIDTOWN · ROPPONGI · ROPPONGI HILLS · NISHI-AZABU · AZABU-JŪBAN · MOTO-AZABU · Arisugawa-no-miya Memorial Park · Shiba-kō · ITORANOMO · National Park for Nature Study · Koishik Kōrak · Palace Ground

Asakusa and around p.52.
Asakusa is Central Tokyo's most traditional area, with temples and shrines surrounded by craft shops, while Ryōgoku comes to life every four months, when the sumo circus rolls into town.

Akihabara and around p.40.
If you're into robots, electronics, *anime*, *manga*, "maid cafés" or anything similar, this is your place – Tokyo doesn't get much quirkier than this madcap area.

Ginza and around p.32.
Famed for its shops, Ginza's grid of streets is highly atmospheric, exuding the worn feel of Tokyo's 1980s bubble period.

The Imperial Palace and around p.24.
The centre of the world's biggest city is surprisingly green and open – a gentle introduction to Tokyo, and great walking territory.

Bayside Tokyo p.60.
With Tokyo so large, it's easy to forget that the city lies by the ocean; breathe in the sea air of the man-made islands dotting its bay area.

15

Things not to miss

It's not possible to see everything that Tokyo has to offer in one trip – and we don't suggest you try. What follows is a selective taste of the city's highlights, from bustling bars to the very best of traditional theatre.

> **Asakusa**
See page 52
Home to old craft shops, traditional inns and the atmospheric Sensō-ji.

< **Sumo**
See page 57
Witness the titanic clashes of wrestling giants at the National Sumo Stadium in Ryōgoku.

∨ **National Art Center**
See page 65
Set aside a chunk of time to explore this enormous gallery, a highlight of the so-called Roppongi Art Triangle.

⟨ Sushi
See page 177
There are innumerable places in which to scoff delectable raw fish – don't leave without giving it a try.

⌄ Matsuri
See page 127
Your visit may well coincide with one of the capital's umpteen *matsuri* (traditional festivals) – a slice of quintessential Japan.

< **Traditional performing arts**
See page 29
Enjoy kabuki, nō and *bunraku*
puppetry at the National Theatre,
Kabukiza Theatre or Shinbashi
Enbujō.

∨ **Rikugi-en**
See page 105
A quintessential Japanese-style
garden designed to reflect scenes
from ancient Japanese poetry.

THINGS NOT TO MISS

∧ Golden Gai
See page 97
It's amazing how many bars are squeezed into this corner of neon-soaked Kabukichō – getting to and from your seat can resemble a game of Twister.

< Hanami parties
See page 128
Pack a picnic and sit under the cherry blossoms in Ueno Park, around the Imperial Palace moat or along the Meguro-gawa.

∧ **Onsen bathing**
See page 62
Soak in an old neighbourhood bathhouse such as the resort-like spa complex of Ōedo Onsen Monogatari in Tokyo Bay.

∨ **Meiji-jingū**
See page 78
Enjoy one of the many annual festivals or regular wedding ceremonies held at Tokyo's most venerable Shinto shrine.

∧ Harajuku
See page 78
Trawl the boutiques of Cat Street, dive into crowded Takeshita-dōri or simply sit and watch the weekend human circus spool by outside Harajuku station.

< Ghibli Museum
See page 98
Most visitors will have seen at least one Studio Ghibli anime – get behind the scenes at this imaginative museum.

< **Nezu Museum**
See page 82
Housed in one of Tokyo's most
impressive pieces of modern
architecture, this repository
of Asian arts also has a
magnificent garden.

∨ **Water buses**
See page 122
Cruise down the Sumida-gawa
or across Tokyo Bay on one of
the city's ferry services, including
the manga-inspired *Himiko*
sightseeing boat.

Day one in Tokyo

Shinjuku Perhaps the most famous Tokyo neighbourhood of all, a high-rise, high-octane mishmash of pulsating neon, teeming crowds and hundreds upon hundreds of bars and restaurants. See page 92

Harajuku See the city's most colourful youngsters dressed up to the nines in outlandish attire. See page 78

🍴 **Lunch** Pause for *tonkatsu* at *Maisen*, then head over to Shibuya station to watch the sheer number of people making their way across the road when the traffic lights change. See page 88

Ginza Head east from the newly revamped Tokyo station and you're in this classic shopping neighbourhood. See page 32

Akihabara Famed as the capital's capital of electronics, head here to get your fix of arcade games, maid cafés, manga-character stores and much more – then stop for dinner at somewhere delicious like *Hachimaki*. See page 40

Ueno Stroll around Ueno Park's lily-filled lake, visit the zoo, experience a couple of temples and gardens, or hit up a few excellent museums. See page 46

Ikebukuro Though off the regular tourist radar, there's plenty to like about Ikebukuro – nearby sights include a retro-futurist cathedral, several onsen and one of architect Frank Lloyd Wright's most famous creations. See page 104

Asakusa Learn all about the history of Tokyo at the staggeringly spacious Edo-Tokyo Museum, filled with mock landmarks, holograms and ancient maps. End your day with a wander around Fukagawa Fudō-dō or through the pleasant gardens of Kiyosumi. See page 55

Shinjuku

Harajuku fashion

Maisen

Day two in Tokyo

Tokyo Metropolitan Government Building This twin-towered beast is one of the most astonishing looking buildings in the otherworldly neon craziness of Shinjuku. Head to its lofty observation decks for one of Tokyo's best views. See page 92

Coffee Enjoy a coffee served by cartoon-character-costumed maids at *Maidreamin* in the neon-drenched mega-district of Shibuya. See page 44

Harajuku shops Kit yourself out in the latest weird and wonderful Tokyo styles along fun, hip shopping alleys such as Takeshita-dōri's, and other quirky shops. See page 84

Senso-ji This stand-out temple is a must-visit on any visitor to Tokyo's itinerary: it is both peaceful and bustling, colourful and quaint, and shouldn't be missed. See page 52

Contemporary art Top-rate galleries abound across the capital, with a particularly strong concentration of small, independent affairs in the Ginza and Roppongi neighbourhoods. See pages 32 and 65

Dinner It would spoil the surprise to describe the wacky performance venue that is *Robot Restaurant* in full. Pop along for an evening show and see what all the fuss is about. See page 98

Karaoke Japan blessed the world with this wonderful concept, so it would be a pity to leave the country without letting it hear your own crimes against music. See page 91

Jicoo Take an evening trip down to Tokyo Bay on this space-age floating bar. See page 63

View from the Government Building

Robot Restaurant

Karaoke

Traditional Tokyo

From temples to theatre, Tokyo has an abundance of traditional experiences to enjoy. Get stuck right in – here are a few of our top selections.

Hot springs If you're willing to bare all to total strangers, Tokyo is a great place to do it – there are several great bathhouses dotted around the city. See page 106

Sensō-ji This charming temple is the focus of the traditional Asakusa neighbourhood; try to visit it in the early evening, since the illuminations come on after sundown. See page 52

Traditional gardens A whole host of immaculately sculpted gardens keep things natural amid the all-pervasive high-rise, with Rikugi-en a particularly appealing example. See page 105

Sensō-ji

Yushima Seidō Just west of Akihabara, this black-laquered shrine receives relatively few visitors, but scores highly on the atmosphere front. See page 43

Izakaya These traditional drinking dens also function as superbly atmospheric places to eat and make new friends. Try sticks of *yakitori* and wash it down with sake or a cold beer. See page 38

Traditional theatre Pop along to Kabukiza Theatre for a spellbinding kabuki performance. See page 33

Yushima Seidō

Japan Traditional Craft Centre Based in Akasaka, head along to this craft centre to buy a pair of chopsticks, lacquerware and more. See page 69

Nezu Museum This prestigious museum features celebrated collections of Oriental treasures, and splendid gardens with several traditional teahouses dotted about. See page 82

Kabukiza Theatre

Eat and drink Tokyo

Eat and drink your way around the city, and you won't be disappointed. From grilled octopus and hearty ramen to craft beer and sake, Tokyo is a real odyssey for your tastebuds.

Tsukemen Tokyo's own creation, these springy noodles are served lukewarm, and then dipped into and slurped from a side bowl of broth. Try them at *Konjiki Hototogisu*. See page 101

Okonomiyaki A kind of savoury pancake filled with whatever ingredients you fancy, cooked up on a hot-plate at your table. Foreigners can learn the ropes at *Sakuratei*. See page 89

Tempura Deep-fried comestibles have been elevated into an art form in Japan; see what all the fuss is about at *Tsunahachi*. See page 101

Tsukemen

Ryokan breakfasts Perhaps the best thing about staying at a ryokan – a traditional Japanese inn – is the delectable breakfast usually plonked in front of you in the morning. See page 112

Sake This Japanese rice-booze is a delight to drink in all its forms: head to an *izakaya* and have it served hot; take your pick of the stylish range of "cup sake" jars on offer at a specialist bar like *Buri* (see page 77); or select one of the beautiful sake bottles on sale at any convenience store.

Okonomiyaki

Craft beer You may not think of Tokyo, or Japan itself, as particularly beer-focused, but there are a number of decent craft breweries dotted around the capital that are worth a glass of *biiru* at. See page 90

Ramen Slurp your way through the ramen joints of Tokyo – *Ramen Kokugikan* has to be one of the best spots. See page 90

Sake collection

PLACES

Kitanomaru-kōen

The Imperial Palace and around

Wrapped round with moats and broad avenues, the enigmatic Imperial Palace lies at the city's geographical and spiritual heart. The palace itself – home to the emperor and his family since 1868 – is closed to the public, but the surrounding parks are a natural place to start any exploration of Tokyo. The most attractive is Higashi Gyoen, where remnants of the old Edo Castle still stand amid formal gardens; to its north lies Kitanomaru-kōen, a more natural park containing a collection of museums, including the excellent National Museum of Modern Art. Look east from the Imperial Palace area and you'll see that the flat parkland on its periphery is, almost immediately, punctuated by a wall of high-rise – this is Marunouchi (literally meaning "inside the circle"), whose crowded streets are transformed at dusk into neon-lit canyons, lined with many of Tokyo's swankiest places to eat, drink and sleep.

The Imperial Palace

MAP P.26, POCKET MAP G6
皇居, Entrance off Uchibori-dōri.
Sakuradamon or Nijūbashimae stations.

Higashi Gyoen

Access by official tour only; apply online and bring your passport. ☎ 03 3213 1111, ⓦ sankan.kunaicho.go.jp. Tues–Sat 10am & 1.30pm, 75min. Free.

The site of the **Imperial Palace** is as old as Tokyo itself. Edo Castle was built here by Tokugawa Ieyasu in 1497, and its boundaries fluctuated through the following centuries. The main citadel lay in today's **Higashi Gyoen** (East Garden; see page 25), and this was surrounded by moats, watchtowers and ramparts spreading over several kilometres. Little remains today, save for three fortified towers, some massive stone walls, and expanses of spruce lawns and manicured pine trees.

The actual imperial **residences**, built in the early 1990s, are tucked away out of sight in the thickly wooded western section of the grounds, surrounded by a protective moat. Admission to the **palace grounds** is only on prearranged **official tours**, which are a bit of a hassle to get on, but provide a fascinating peek inside this secret world.

Higashi Gyoen

MAP P.26, POCKET MAP G6
東御苑, **East entrance off Uchibori-dōri,
north entrance opposite National Museum
of Modern Art. Ōtemachi or Takebashi
stations. Tues–Thurs, Sat & Sun 9am–4pm
(closed occasionally for court functions).
Free tokens issued at park entrance; hand
back on exit.**

Hemmed in by moats, the **Higashi
Gyoen**, or East Garden, was
opened to the public in 1968 to
commemorate the completion
of the new Imperial Palace, and
is a good place for a stroll. The
towering granite walls, as well as
several formidable gates, hint at
the grandeur of the shogunate's
Edo Castle, part of which stood
here until being consumed by a
catastrophic fire in the seventeenth
century. The main gate to the
garden is **Ōte-mon**, an austere,
moat-side construction whose
bottom half is made up of
charmingly wonky cubes of rock;
further on, the finest of the fortress's
remaining watchtowers is the
three-tiered **Fujimi-yagura**, built in
1659 to protect the main citadel's
southern flank. These days it rises
above the Higashi Gyoen like a
miniature version of the old castle
itself, standing clear above the trees
to the north of the Imperial Plaza.

Kitanomaru-kōen

MAP P.26, POCKET MAP F5
北の丸公園, **North entrance off
Yasukuni-dōri. Kudanshita or Takebashi
stations. 24hr. Free.**
Edo Castle's old northern citadel
is now occupied by the park
of **Kitanomaru-kōen**. With
its ninety-odd cherry trees, it's
a popular viewing spot come
hanami time, while rowing boats
can be rented in warmer months
on **Chidoriga-fuchi**, an ancient
pond once incorporated into Edo
Castle's moat.

National Museum of Modern Art

MAP P.26, POCKET MAP G5
国立近代美術館, **Tues–Sun
10am–5pm, Fri & Sat 10am–8pm.** ☎ 03
5777 8600, 🌐 momat.go.jp. **¥500, or ¥300
after 5pm Fri & Sat; extra fees apply for
special exhibitions.**

Descendants of the Sun Goddess

The previous emperor, **Akihito** (the 125th incumbent of the
Chrysanthemum Throne), traced his ancestry back to 660 BC and
Emperor Jimmu, great-great-grandson of the mythological Sun
Goddess Amaterasu. Most scholars, however, acknowledge that
the first emperor for whom there is any historical evidence is the
fifth-century Emperor Ojin.

Until the twentieth century, emperors were regarded as living
deities whom ordinary folk were forbidden to set eyes on, or
even hear. Japan's defeat in World War II ended all that and
today the emperor is a symbolic figure, a head of state with no
governmental power. While he was crown prince, **Akihito** broke
with tradition by marrying a commoner, **Shōda Michiko**; his son,
Naruhito, who is now the current Emperor, followed suit in 1993
by marrying Harvard-educated diplomat Owada Masako.

In August 2016, Akihito gave only his second-ever televised
address, mentioning his health problems and advancing age,
and hinting at an extremely rare Japanese abdication. This duly
came to pass in 2019, when he handed over the Chrysanthemum
Throne to its 126th incumbent, son Naruhito, thus ushering in the
Reiwa period.

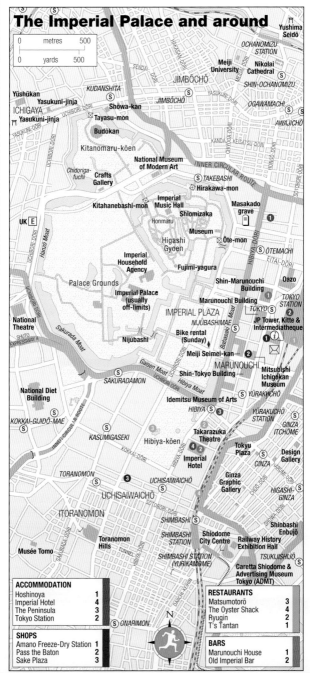

The Imperial Palace and around

ACCOMMODATION	
Hoshinoya	1
Imperial Hotel	4
The Peninsula	3
Tokyo Station	2

SHOPS	
Amano Freeze-Dry Station	1
Pass the Baton	2
Sake Plaza	3

RESTAURANTS	
Matsumotorō	3
The Oyster Shack	4
Ryugin	2
T's Tantan	1

BARS	
Marunouchi House	1
Old Imperial Bar	2

Strewn over three large levels, the **National Museum of Modern Art**'s excellent permanent collection showcases Japanese art since 1900, as well as a few pieces of work from overseas; the former includes Gyokudo Kawai's magnificent screen painting *Parting Spring* and works by Kishida Ryūsei, Fujita Tsuguharu and postwar artists such as Yoshihara Jiro. On the fourth floor you'll find the earliest works, as well as a resting area with fantastic views over the moat and palace grounds; the third floor contains perhaps the most interesting section, featuring art made either during wartime or its aftermath.

Crafts Gallery

MAP P.26, POCKET MAP F5

工芸館, Tues–Sun 10am–5pm. ☎ 03 5777 8600, ⓦ momat.go.jp. ¥210; usually ¥900 for special exhibitions.

Tucked away on the west side of Kitanomaru-kōen, the **Crafts Gallery** exhibits a selection of top-quality traditional Japanese craft works, many by modern masters. Erected in 1910 as the headquarters of the Imperial Guards, this neo-Gothic red-brick pile is one of very few Tokyo buildings dating from before the Great Earthquake of 1923 – it looks like the kind of place Harry Potter would have gone to school, had he been Japanese.

Shōwa-kan

MAP P.26, POCKET MAP F5

昭和館, Off Yasukuni-dōri. Kudanshita station. Tues–Sun 10am–5.30pm. ☎ 03 3222 2577, ⓦ www.showakan.go.jp. ¥300; English-language audio-guides free.

There is something more than a little creepy about the **Shōwa-kan**, a museum devoted to life in Japan during and after World War II. It's almost as if the designers of this windowless corrugated building were acknowledging the secrecy that surrounds what really happened in those years – take a

Yasukuni Jinja

look at the exhibits and you'll see scarcely a mention of bombs or destruction. However, there's some interesting material concerning life during the occupation in the sixth- and seventh-floor exhibition rooms, including empty hacky sacks from which starving children ate the dried beans used as stuffing.

Yasukuni-jinja

MAP P.26, POCKET MAP F5

靖国神社, Entrance off Yasukuni-dōri. Kudanshita or Ichigaya stations. ⓦ yasukuni.or.jp. Daily: March–Oct 6am–6pm, Nov–Feb 6am–5pm. Free.

A monumental red steel *torii* marks the entrance to **Yasukuni-jinja**, a shrine founded in 1869 to worship supporters of the emperor killed in the run-up to the Meiji Restoration. Since then it has expanded to include the legions sacrificed in subsequent wars, in total nearly 2.5 million souls, of whom some two million died in the Pacific War alone; the parting words of kamikaze pilots were said to be "see you at Yasukuni". Every year some eight million Japanese visit this shrine, which controversially includes several war

Yūshūkan (military museum)

criminals; security has been tight since a minor explosion here in late 2015.

Standing at the end of a long avenue lined with cherry and ginkgo trees and accessed through a simple wooden gate, the architecture is classic Shintō styling, solid and unadorned except for two gold imperial chrysanthemums embossed on the main doors. If this is all surprisingly unassuming, the same cannot be said for a couple of menacing metal lanterns near the entrance, whose distinctive Rising Sun-like patterns are most evident at dusk.

Yūshūkan

MAP P.26, POCKET MAP F5
遊就館, ☎ 03 3261 8326. Daily
9am–4.30pm. ¥1000.
Within Yasukuni-jinja you'll find the **Yūshūkan**, a military museum whose displays are well presented, but gloss over events such as the Nanking Massacre and other atrocities by Japanese troops; the Pacific War is presented as a war of liberation, freeing the peoples of Southeast Asia from Western colonialism. The most moving displays are the ranks of faded photographs and the "bride dolls" donated by the families of young soldiers who died before they were married.

Mitsubishi Ichigokan Museum

MAP P.26, POCKET MAP H6
三菱一号館美術館, 2-6-2
Marunouchi. Tokyo or Nijūbashimae
stations. ☎ 03 5405 8686, 🌐 mimt.jp.
Daily 10am–6pm, Fri and final week of each exhibition until 9pm. Price depends on exhibition – usually ¥1700, with ¥200 discount to foreign tourists with ID.
Worth a look for its design as much as its contents, the **Mitsubishi Ichigokan Museum** is housed in a meticulous reconstruction of a red-brick office block designed by British architect Josiah Conder; the

original was erected on the same site in 1894, only to be demolished in 1968. Exhibitions rotate every four months or so, and almost exclusively focus on nineteenth-century European art, usually of a pretty high calibre.

Intermediatheque

MAP P.26, POCKET MAP H6

インターメディアテク, 2–3F Kitte Building, 2-7-2 Marunouchi. Tokyo station. ☏ 03 5777 8600, ⓦ intermediatheque. jp. Mon–Thurs & Sun 11am–6pm, Fri & Sat 11am–8pm; closed a few days per month. Free.

The double-level **Intermediatheque** is, without doubt, one of the most intriguing museum spaces in the city, hosting exhibitions that are sharply curated and pieced together with a rare attention to aesthetic detail. The permanent exhibition is a well-presented mishmash of various objects of scientific and cultural heritage accumulated by the Tokyo University; the animal skeletons are the most eye-catching exhibits, but poke around and you'll find everything from Central American headwear to objects damaged by the nuclear explosions in Nagasaki.

Idemitsu Museum of Arts

MAP P.26, POCKET MAP G7

出光美術館 , 9F Teigeki Building, 3-1-1 Marunouchi. Hibiya or Yūrakuchō stations. ☏ 03 5777 8600, ⓦ idemitsu-museum. or.jp. Tues–Sun 10am–5pm, Fri until 7pm. ¥1000.

Sitting above the Imperial Theatre, the **Idemitsu Museum of Arts** houses a magnificent assortment of mostly Japanese art, though only a tiny proportion is on show at any one time. The collection includes many historically important pieces, ranging from fine examples of early Jōmon (10,000 BC–300 BC) pottery to Zen Buddhist calligraphy, hand-painted scrolls, richly gilded folding screens and elegant, late seventeenth-century *ukiyo-e* paintings. The museum also owns valuable collections of Chinese and Korean ceramics.

National Theatre

MAP P.26, POCKET MAP F6

国立劇場, 4-1 Hayabusachō. Hanzōmon station. ☏ 03 3230 3000, ⓦ www.ntj.jac. go.jp.

In its two auditoria, Tokyo's National Theatre puts on a varied programme of traditional theatre and music, including kabuki, *bunraku*, court music and dance. English-language earphones and programmes are available. Tickets start at around ¥1500 for kabuki and ¥4500 for *bunraku*.

Takarazuka Theatre

MAP P.26, POCKET MAP G7

1-1-3 Yūrakuchō. Hibiya station. ☏ 03 5251 2001, ⓦ kageki.hankyu.co.jp.

Mostly stages musicals, punched out by a huge cast in fabulous costumes. The theatre, immediately north of the *Imperial Hotel*, also stages regular Takarazuka performances. Tickets start at ¥3500; performances run most days (except Wed) at either 11am or 1pm, and at 3pm.

Mitsubishi Ichigokan Museum

Shops

Amano Freeze-Dry Station

MAP P.26, POCKET MAP H6
B1F Kitte Building, 2-7-2 Marunouchi. Tokyo station. ☎ 03 6256 0911. Daily 10am–8pm.
A fun little shop for freeze-dried food – take some soups, curries or risotto home, then dine like a Japanese astronaut.

Pass the Baton

MAP P.26, POCKET MAP G7
Brick Square, 2-6-1 Marunouchi. Tokyo station. ☎ 03 6269 9555. Mon–Sat 11am–9pm, Sun until 8pm.
This curate's egg of a shop is like a boutique recycling store, with carefully chosen decorative objects and fashion items.

Sake Plaza

MAP P.26, POCKET MAP G7
酒プラザー, 1-1-21 Nishi-Shinbashi.

Matsumotorō

Toranomon or Uchisai-wachō stations.
☎ 03 3519 2091. Mon–Fri 10am–6pm.
Shop and tasting room with an excellent range of sake from all over the country; those on offer change daily.

Restaurants

Matsumotorō

MAP P.26, POCKET MAP G7
1-2 Hibiya-kōen. Hibiya station. ☎ 03 3503 1451, ⌨ matsumotoro.co.jp. Daily 10am–9pm.
On a sunny day it's a pleasure to sit on the terrace of this venerable park restaurant. Food is along the lines of omu-raisu (rice-filled omelette; ¥1400), hamburgers and other Western "favourites".

The Oyster Shack

MAP P.26, POCKET MAP G8
1-6-1 Uchisaiwai-chō. Shimbashi station.

Vegan ramen at T's Tantan

🕿 03 6205 4328, Ⓦ kakigoya.jimdo.
com. Mon–Fri 4–11.30pm, Sat & Sun
noon–11pm.
One of the city's most atmospheric
oyster bars, snuggled under
train track arches. Oysters cost
from ¥300, and there's a whole
aquarium's worth of other stuff to
slurp down.

Ryugin

MAP P.26, POCKET MAP G7
Tokyo Midtown Hibiya, 1-1-2 Yurakuchō.
Hibiya station. 🕿 03 6630 0007, Ⓦ www.
nihonryori-ryugin.com. Daily 5.30–11pm.
Voted among the world's top
restaurants on several occasions,
this is a prime place for a kaiseki
meal, given a twist of molecular
gastronomy. At around ¥40,000 or
so, it's not cheap; think Hokkaido
lamb, Honshu pheasant, Ezo deer
and other seasonal dishes.

T's Tantan

MAP P.26, POCKET MAP H6
たんたん, Keiyo Street, 1-9-1
Marunouchi. Tokyo station. 🕿 03
3218 8040, Ⓦ ts-restaurant.jp. Daily
7am–10.30pm.
Vegan ramen – a great idea.
The spicy, drier *tantan-men* is
even better (¥850), while they

also have vegan *gyōza* and spicy
tofu. It's actually located inside
Tokyo station.

Bars and clubs

Marunouchi House

MAP P.26, POCKET MAP H6
7F Shin-Marunouchi Bldg, 1-5-1
Maranouchi. Tokyo station. 🕿 03
5218 5100. Mon–Sat 11am–4am, Sun
11am–11pm.
The best thing about the open-plan
space here, with its seven different
restaurants and bars, is that you
can take your drinks out on to the
broad wraparound terrace for great
views of Tokyo station and towards
the Imperial Palace.

Old Imperial Bar

MAP P.26, POCKET MAP G7
Imperial Hotel, 1-1-1 Uchisaiwaichō.
Hibiya station. 🕿 03 3539 8088, Ⓦ www.
imperialhotel.co.jp. Daily 11.30am–midnight.
All that remains of Frank Lloyd
Wright's Art Deco *Imperial Hotel*;
try the signature Mount Fuji
cocktail (¥1800), a wickedly sweet
blend of gin, cream, egg white and
sugar syrup with a cherry on top,
which was invented here in 1924.

Ginza and around

Ginza, the "place where silver is minted", took its name after Shogun Tokugawa Ieyasu started making coins here in the early 1600s. It turned into a happy association: one street, Chūō-dōri, soon grew to become Japan's most stylish shopping thoroughfare. Although now a couple of decades past its heyday, the glut of luxury malls and flagship stores here remains the envy of Tokyo, while various bars, restaurants and cafés still reverberate with distinct echoes of the "bubble period", a time in which Tokyo itself was the envy of the rest of the world. This slice of quintessential modern-day Japan is fascinating enough, but add a sprinkling of great museums and galleries, and you're set for the day, especially when you factor in the sights of the neighbouring districts of Nihombashi and Shiodome, which bookend Ginza to north and south.

Advertising Museum Tokyo

MAP P.34, POCKET MAP H8
広告とマーケティングの資料館,
B1 Caretta Shiodome. Shiodome station.
☎ 03 62182500, ⓦ admt.jp. Tues–Sat
11am–6pm. Free.

Hama Rikyū Onshi Teien

In the basement of the **Caretta Shiodome** skyscraper – the sleek headquarters of the Dentsu ad agency – you'll find **Advertising Museum Tokyo (ADMT)**, a small permanent exhibition providing a fascinating flick through some of the twentieth century's most arresting commercial images, including a decade-by-decade look at Japanese product design and advertising.

Hama Rikyū Onshi Teien

MAP P.34, POCKET MAP G9
浜離宮恩賜庭園, 1-1
Hamarikyūteien. Shiodome station. Daily
9am–4.30pm. ¥300; tea ¥510.
The beautifully designed traditional garden of **Hama Rikyū Onshi Teien** once belonged to the shogunate, who hunted ducks here. Next to the entrance is a sprawling, 300-year-old pine tree and a manicured lawn dotted with sculpted, stunted trees. There are three ponds, the largest spanned by a trellis-covered bridge that leads to a floating teahouse; in early

spring lilac wisteria hangs in fluffy bunches from trellises around the central pond.

Kabukiza Theatre

MAP P.34, POCKET MAP H7
歌舞伎座, 4-12-15 Ginza. Higashi-Ginza station. Ⓦ kabuki-za.co.jp. Gallery open daily 11am–7pm. Free.

Tokyo rejoiced when the famed **Kabukiza Theatre**, one of Ginza's most iconic buildings, reopened its doors in early 2013. First opened in 1889, the theatre has been rebuilt several times, a victim of fires and war damage. The architect behind its most recent incarnation is Kengo Kuma, who reinstated the elaborate facade of the original, which burned down in 1921; backed by a modern 29-storey office block, this is classic "city of contrasts" territory. While anyone can check out the fifth-floor gallery, with its wonderful display of kabuki costumes, you can't beat actually watching a play here – getting a ticket (¥4000–22,000) can be tricky, but usually becomes easier after the fifteenth of each month. Single-act tickets (¥800–2000) are available on the door for those who don't want to commit to a whole performance.

Kabukiza Theatre

Shinbashi Enbujō

MAP P.34, POCKET MAP H8
6-18-2 Ginza. Higashi-Ginza station. Ⓣ 03 3541 2600, Ⓦ shinbashi-enbujo.co.jp.

This large **theatre** stages a range of traditional dance, music and theatre, including the "Super-kabuki" (kabuki with all the bells and whistles of modern musical theatre). Single-act tickets for regular kabuki performances range from ¥800 to ¥1500 depending on the length of the act.

Ginza glitz

Much of the credit for **Ginza**'s unusually regular pattern of streets can go to British architect Thomas Waters, who was given the task of creating a less combustible city after a fire in 1872 destroyed virtually all of old, wooden Ginza. His "Bricktown", as it soon became known, proved an instant local tourist attraction, with its rows of two-storey brick houses, tree-lined avenues, gaslights and brick pavements.

Most of the first businesses here dealt in foreign wares, and in no time Ginza became the centre of all that was modern and Western – and, by extension, fashionable. Bricktown itself fell down in the Great Earthquake of 1923, but by then Ginza's status was well established. In the 1930s the height of sophistication was simply to stroll around Ginza, and the practice still continues, particularly on Sunday afternoons, when Chūō-dōri is closed to traffic and everyone turns out for a spot of window-shopping.

Ginza and around

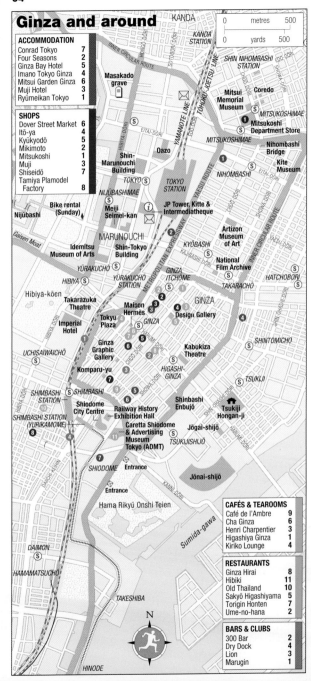

ACCOMMODATION
Conrad Tokyo	7
Four Seasons	2
Ginza Bay Hotel	5
Imano Tokyo Ginza	4
Mitsui Garden Ginza	6
Muji Hotel	3
Ryūmeikan Tokyo	1

SHOPS
Dover Street Market	6
Itō-ya	4
Kyūkyodō	5
Mikimoto	2
Mitsukoshi	1
Muji	3
Shiseidō	7
Tamiya Plamodel Factory	8

CAFÉS & TEAROOMS
Café de l'Ambre	9
Cha Ginza	6
Henri Charpentier	3
Higashiya Ginza	1
Kiriko Lounge	4

RESTAURANTS
Ginza Hirai	8
Hibiki	11
Old Thailand	10
Sakyō Higashiyama	5
Torigin Honten	7
Ume-no-hana	2

BARS & CLUBS
300 Bar	2
Dry Dock	4
Lion	3
Marugin	1

Maison Hermès

MAP P.34, POCKET MAP H7
8F 5-4-1 Ginza. Ginza station. ☎ 03 3569
3611, ⓦ maisonhermes.jp/ginza. Daily
11am–7pm.

Possibly the most charming gallery
space in all Tokyo, **Maison Hermès**
is set at the top of the Renzo Piano-
designed "bubble-wrap" building
that's home to the high-end fashion
behemoth's Tokyo boutique. Worth
a look whatever the exhibit – the
gallery usually hosts themed shows
of Japanese and international art.

Komparu-yu

MAP P.34, POCKET MAP G8
金春湯, 8-7-5 Ginza. Ginza station.
Mon–Sat 2–10pm. ¥460, plus ¥130 for a
towel.

One of the most central bathhouses
in Tokyo, little **Komparu-yu** is
a great little place to stop off for
a scrub while touring Ginza. It's
cheap, and suits the area nicely (as
it should, having been here since
1863), with the decor featuring the
near-obligatory Mount Fuji mural
as well as other tiling depicting
flowers, animals and the like. All in
all, it's a lovely experience.

Artizon Museum of Art

MAP P.34, POCKET MAP H7
1-10-1 Kyōbashi. Tokyo, Kyōbashi or
Nihombashi stations. ☎ 03 3563 0241,
ⓦ bridgestone-museum.gr.jp.

The Bridgestone Museum of Art
was renamed the **Artizon Museum
of Art** and is due to reopen in early
2020. The museum is home to an
impressive collection of paintings
by Van Gogh, Renoir, Degas,
Monet, Manet, Miró, Picasso
and other heavyweights, as well
as Meiji-era Japanese paintings
in Western style – it's well worth
swinging by.

Mitsui Memorial Museum

MAP P.34, POCKET MAP H6
三井記念美術館, 7F Mitsui Main
Building, 2-1-1 Nihombashi Muromachi.
Mitsukoshimae station. ☎ 03 5777 8600,
ⓦ mitsui-museum.jp. Tues–Sun 10am–5pm.
¥1000, or ¥1300 for special exhibitions.

Just north of the main branch of
the Mitsukoshi department store
(see page 34), wood-panelled
lifts rise to the seventh-floor **Mitsui
Memorial Museum**, where a
superb collection spanning three
hundred years of Japanese and
Asian art is on display. Exhibitions
follow a seasonal theme, and are
mostly aimed at the connoisseur
– you'll often see older Tokyoites
purring with pleasure at the
pottery, calligraphy, jades or
jewellery before them.

Maison Hermès

Shops

Dover Street Market

MAP P.34, POCKET MAP H7

6-9-6 Ginza. Ginza station. ☎ 03 6228
5080, Ⓦ ginza.doverstreetmarket.com.
Mon–Sat 11am–8pm.

The several floors here feature
clothing from almost every major
Japanese designer, without the
department-store atmosphere that
usually goes with such choice.

Itō-ya

MAP P.34, POCKET MAP H7

2-7-15 Ginza. Shibuya station. ☎ 03
3561 8311, Ⓦ ito-ya.co.jp. Mon–Sat
10.30am–8pm, Sun 10.30am–7pm.

Fabulous stationery store
comprising 11 floors and two
annexes: a treasure-trove full
of packable souvenirs such as
traditional *washi* paper, calligraphy
brushes, inks and so on.

Kyūkyodō

MAP P.34, POCKET MAP H7

5-7-4 Ginza. Ginza station. ☎ 03 3571
4429. Daily 10am–7pm.

Filled with the dusty smell of
sumi-e ink, this venerable shop
has been selling traditional
paper, calligraphy brushes and
inkstones since 1800. During Edo
times, they provided incense to
the emperor.

Mikimoto

MAP P.34, POCKET MAP H7

4-5-5 Ginza. Ginza station. ☎ 03 3535
4611, Ⓦ www.mikimoto.com. Daily
11am–7pm.

The famous purveyor of cultured
pearls has branched out into
diamonds and other jewellery lines,
all shown off to perfection in its
dramatic main store in the heart
of Ginza.

Mitsukoshi

MAP P.34, POCKET MAP H6

1-4-1 Nihombashi-Muromachi.
Mitsukoshimae station. ☎ 03 3241 3311.
Daily 10.30am–7.30pm.

Mitsukoshi department store

Tokyo's most prestigious and oldest department store – dating back to 1673 – is elegant, spacious and renowned for its high-quality merchandise.

Muji

MAP P.34, POCKET MAP H7

3-3-5 Ginza. Shinjuku station. ☎ 03 5367 2710. Daily 10am–9pm.

One of the newest and biggest branches of this homeware, lifestyle and fashion chain, a "no-brand" concept whose logo is now, ironically, seen across the world. Other branches around the city.

Shiseidō

MAP P.34, POCKET MAP G8

8-8-3 Ginza. Ginza or Shimbashi stations. ☎ 03 3572 3913, ⓦ shiseido.co.jp. Mon–Sat 11.30am–7.30pm, Sun 11.30am–7pm.

One of the oldest and largest cosmetics companies in the world, *Shiseidō* was established in Tokyo in 1872, and their main branch occupies a distinctive red building.

Tamiya Plamodel Factory

MAP P.34, POCKET MAP G8

4-7-2 Shimbashi. Shimbashi station. ☎ 03 3719 8124, ⓦ tamiya-plamodelfactory.co.jp. Mon–Fri noon–10pm, Sat & Sun noon–6pm.

Model-kit enthusiasts rejoice – the Japanese manufacturer's entire range is available in this three-level emporium, showcasing thousands of scale and radio-controlled models.

Cafés and tearooms

Café de l'Ambre

MAP P.34, POCKET MAP G8

8-10-15 Ginza. Shimbashi station. ☎ 03 3571 1551. Mon & Wed–Sat noon–9.30pm, Sun noon–6.30pm.

One of Tokyo's best coffee venues, this old-school Ginza *kissaten* has been roasting beans since the 1950s, achieving something approaching coffee perfection in

Shiseidō

the intervening years. Most cups (from ¥700) are made with a cotton-felt filter.

Cha Ginza

MAP P.34, POCKET MAP H7

5-5-6 Ginza. Ginza station. ☎ 03 3571 1211. Daily (except Mon) 11am–6pm.

Contemporary teahouse, a place to hang out with those Tokyo ladies who make shopping a career. ¥700 gets you three small cups of the refreshing green stuff, plus a traditional sweet.

Henri Charpentier

MAP P.34, POCKET MAP H7

2-8-20 Ginza. Ginza-itchōme station. ☎ 03 3562 2721, ⓦ henri-charpentier.com. Daily 11am–9pm.

Deep-pink boutique patisserie and *salon de thé*, where you can enjoy crêpe suzette (¥2500, including a drink), flambéed at your table, as well as a range of gold-flecked chocolate morsels and seasonal specialities.

Higashiya Ginza

MAP P.34, POCKET MAP H7

2F Pola Ginza, 1-7-7 Ginza. Ginza station.

300 Bar

📞 03 3538 3230. Daily 11am–9pm.
This utterly gorgeous tearoom
and shop is known for its relaxing
atmosphere and delicious
assortments of seasonal Japanese
sweets (from ¥1500); the tea itself
goes from a pricey ¥1700 per head,
though a pot will be enough for
three cups.

Kiriko Lounge

MAP P.34, POCKET MAP H7
6F Tokyo Tokyu Plaza 5-2-1 Ginza. Ginza
station. 📞 03 6264 5590. Mon–Sat
11am–11pm, Sun 11am–9pm.
This swanky place allows you to
drain coffee (from ¥700) with
a superlative view of Ginza's
high-rises, through some truly
gigantic windows.

Restaurants

Ginza Hirai

MAP P.34, POCKET MAP H7
5-9-5 Ginza. Higashi-Ginza station. 📞 03
6280 6933. Daily 11.30am–2.30pm &
5.30–10pm.
About as old-school Ginza as you
can get, this is an atmospheric place

to tuck into conger eel on rice.
¥1800 will get you a bowl of the
stuff, plus pickles and miso soup.

Hibiki

MAP P.34, POCKET MAP G8
46F Caretta Shiodome Building, 1-8-1
Higashi-Shinbashi. Shiodome station. 📞 03
6215 8051, 🌐 www.dynac-japan.com/
hibiki. Mon–Fri 11am–3pm & 5–11.30pm,
Sat & Sun 11am–4pm & 5–11pm.
This modern *izakaya* boasts some of
Tokyo's best views, up on the 46th
floor with large windows facing out
over Tokyo Bay. The contemporary
Japanese lunch sets (from ¥1200)
are particularly good value.

Old Thailand

MAP P.34, POCKET MAP G8
2-15-3 Shimbashi. Shimbashi station.
📞 03 6206 1532. Mon–Sat 11.30am–3pm
& 5pm–11pm.
Lively Thai restaurant whose menu
features unusual creations such as
specialities from the northeastern
Isaan region, and delectable Chiang
Mai curry noodles (¥1100).

Sakyō Higashiyama

MAP P.34, POCKET MAP H7
B1F Oak Ginza, 3-7-2 Ginza. Ginza station.
📞 03 3535 3577, 🌐 sakyohigashiyama.com.
Mon–Sat 11.30am–3pm & 5.30–11pm.
Refined *kyō-ryōri* (Kyoto-style
cuisine) is served at this rustic
basement space, decorated
with bamboo. The lunch set
(¥2200) includes six delicious,
seasonal courses.

Torigin Honten

MAP P.34, POCKET MAP H7
5-5-7 Ginza. Ginza station. 📞 03 3571
3333, 🌐 torigin-ginza.co.jp. Daily
11.30am–10pm.
Bright, popular restaurant hidden
away on a side street – look for
the red sign. They serve snacks like
yakitori (from ¥170 per stick) and
kamameshi (kettle-cooked rice with
a choice of toppings; from ¥880).

Ume-no-hana

MAP P.34, POCKET MAP H7

5F 2-3-6 Ginza. Ginza-itchōme station.
☎ 03 3538 2226, ⓦ umenohana.co.jp. Daily
11am–4pm & 5–10pm.
Trickling streams and bamboo
screens set the mood in this elegant
restaurant, specializing in melt-
in-the-mouth tofu creations. Sets
change by the season, but lunch
courses generally go from ¥2100,
while dinner sets start at ¥3560.

Bars and clubs

300 Bar

MAP P.34, POCKET MAP H8
B1 Fazenda Building, 5-9-11 Ginza.
Ginza station. ☎ 03 3572 6300. Mon–Fri
5pm–2am, Sat & Sun 2pm–2am.
The bargain-basement face of
Ginza is this fun standing-only bar,
where all food and drinks are ¥300
(plus a little more, with tax).

Dry Dock

MAP P.34, POCKET MAP G8
3-25-10 Shimbashi. Shimbashi station.
☎ 03 5777 4755. Mon–Fri 5pm–midnight,
Sat 5pm–10pm.

Cosy craft-beer bar nestling
beneath the train tracks. Its
no-smoking policy is a welcome
change, and patrons often spill
outside to enjoy the regularly
changing menu of Japanese and
overseas microbrews.

Lion

MAP P.34, POCKET MAP H8
7-9-20 Ginza. Ginza station. ☎ 03 3571
2590. Mon–Sat 11.30am–11pm, Sun
11.30am–10.30pm.
Opened in 1934, they serve good
draught beer (giant ones ¥1080),
there are sausages, sauerkraut and
other German snacks on offer
alongside international pub grub.

Marugin

MAP P.34, POCKET MAP G7
7-1 Ginza. Ginza station. ☎ 03 3571 8989.
Mon–Fri 5pm–midnight, Sat 5pm–10pm.
Unlike many of the tourist-trap
places abutting the tracks here,
this tachinomiya (standing bar)
is manifestly local, and often
completely packed. Fried sticks go
from ¥130, and booze is cheap.

Lion

Akihabara and around

Up the tracks from the Ginza area, a blaze of adverts and a cacophony of competing audio systems announce Akihabara. "Akiba", as it's popularly known, is Tokyo's foremost discount shopping area for electrical and electronic goods of all kinds, but these days it has also become a hotspot for fans of anime and manga, and is famed as the spawning ground for the decidedly surreal "maid cafés" (see page 41). Though Akiba's buzzing, neon-lit streets are almost entirely dedicated to technological wizardry and pop culture, there are sights of a different nature to the west, including the lively Shintō shrine of Kanda Myōjin, and an austere monument to Confucius at Yushima Seidō.

3331 Arts Chiyoda

MAP P.42, POCKET MAP H4
3331アーツ千代田, 6-11-14 Sotokanda. Suehirochō station. ☏ 03 6803 2441, ⓦ 3331.jp. Daily (except Tues) noon–7pm. Usually free, though charges apply for some special exhibitions.
Based inside a renovated school, **3331 Arts Chiyoda** hosts close to twenty galleries; although some spaces tend towards the twee, a handful of prominent artists have cut their teeth here, and all in all it usually makes for an absorbing look at the Japanese art scene.

Kanda Myōjin

MAP P.42, POCKET MAP H4
神田明神, 2-16-2 Sotokanda. Ochanomizu station. Daily 9am–4pm. Free.

3331 Arts Chiyoda

Kanda Matsuri

A vermilion gate marks the entrance to **Kanda Myōjin**, one of the city's oldest shrines and host to one of its top three festivals, the **Kanda Matsuri**.

Founded in 730 AD, the shrine originally stood in front of Edo Castle, where it was dedicated to the gods of farming and fishing (Daikoku and Ebisu).

Taking the pulse of Akihabara

There are few other Tokyo districts in which so many travellers actually avoid the sights: instead, **contemporary culture** is Akihabara's main, or even exclusive, drawcard. Other than the innumerable electronics stores, including *Laox* (see page 44), it's perhaps most famous for its maid cafés, which come in many different guises: Cosplay maids, schoolgirl maids, sailor maids, kimono maids, and many more. You'll see a bunch of cafés clamouring for custom; one safe bet is *Maidreamin* (see page 44), on the second floor of a building, which boasts seven full levels of maid cafés, and nothing else. *Radio Kaikan* (see page 44) and *Comic Tora-no-ana* (see page 44) are good bets for figurines, films, anime-related clothing, and basically everything in between, while you can also put together a whole robot at *Tsukumo Robot Kingdom* (see page 44). Elsewhere you'll find shops selling capsule toys, mammoth gaming centres such as Taito Station (see page 43), and even a department store for sex toys – happy hunting!

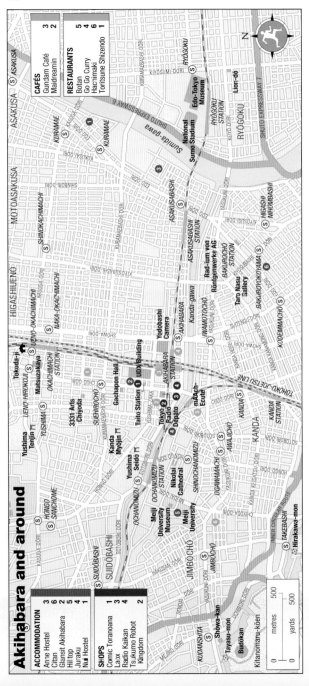

Akihabara and around

ACCOMMODATION	
Anne Hostel	3
Citan	6
Glansit Akihabara	2
Hill top	5
Juraku	4
Nui Hostel	1

SHOPS	
Comic Toranoana	1
Laox	3
Radio Kaikan	4
Tsukumo Robot Kingdom	2

CAFÉS	
Gundam Café	3
Maidreamin	2

RESTAURANTS	
Botan	5
Go Go Curry	4
Hacimaki	6
Toritsune Shizendo	1

Taito Station

MAP P.42, POCKET MAP H4
タイトー白慢, 4-2-2 Sotokanda.
Asakusa station. Daily 10am–midnight.
Free.

If you want to see "crazy" Japan,
Taito Station is a pretty good
place to start. Around the complex
you'll see Tokyoites – and not
just the young ones – perfecting
their moves on dance machines,
thrashing the hell out of
computerized drum kits, playing
all sorts of screen-whacking games,
and using grabbing cranes to pluck
teddies for their dates.

Yushima Seidō

MAP P.42, POCKET MAP H4
湯島聖堂, 1-4-25 Yushima.
Ochanomizu station. Daily: May–Oct
9.30am–5pm, Nov–April 9.30am–4pm.
Free.

A copse of woodland hides the
distinctive shrine of **Yushima
Seidō**, dedicated to the Chinese
sage Confucius. The Seidō (Sacred
Hall) was founded in 1632 as
an academy for the study of the
ancient classics at a time when
the Tokugawa were promoting
Confucianism as the state's ethical
foundation. In 1691 the hall was
moved to its present location,
where it became an elite school
for the sons of samurai and
high-ranking officials, though
most of these buildings were
lost in the fires of 1923. Today,
the quiet compound contains
an eighteenth-century wooden
gate and, at the top of broad
steps, the imposing, black-
lacquered Taisen-den, or "Hall
of Accomplishments", where the
shrine to Confucius is located.

AKIHABARA AND AROUND

Taito Station

Shops

Comic Toranoana

MAP P.42, POCKET MAP H4

4-3-1 Soto-Kanda. Akihabara station. ☎ 03 3526 5330. Daily 10am–10pm.
Seven floors of manga- and anime-related products, including self-published works and secondhand comics on the top floor. There are several other branches across the city.

Laox

MAP P.42, POCKET MAP H4

1-2-9 Soto-Kanda. Akihabara station. ☎ 03 3255 9041. Mon–Fri 10am–8pm, Fri & Sat 10am–9pm.
One of the most prominent names in Akiba and probably the best place to start browsing: you can buy everything from pocket calculators to plasma screen TVs.

Radio Kaikan

MAP P.42, POCKET MAP H4

1-15-16 Soto-Kanda. Akihabara station. Mon–Sat 10.30am–8pm, Sun 10.30am–7.30pm.
Nirvana for *otaku* (obsessive fans), this huge store caters to a rich and varied set of anime and manga tastes – everything from lifelike dolls, figurines and model kits to fantasy and sexually charged items.

Tsukumo Robot Kingdom

MAP P.42, POCKET MAP H4

1-9-9 Soto-Kanda. Akihabara station. ☎ 03 3253 5599. Daily 10am–10pm.
Electrical store selling robot components, with a whole floor aimed at model enthusiasts building their very own androids.

Cafés

Gundam Café

MAP P.42, POCKET MAP H4

1-1 Kanda-Hanaokachō. Akihabara station. ☎ 03 3251 0078, ⓦ g-cafe.jp. Mon–Fri 10am–10pm, Sat 8.30am–11pm, Sun 8.30am–9.20pm.
In the suitably sci-fi interior of this café you can experience what a pilot from the incredibly popular anime series *Mobile Suit Gundam* would eat – or at least our terrestrial equivalent. Coffees from ¥400.

Maidreamin

MAP P.42, POCKET MAP H4

Gundam Café

Botan

2F 1-8-10 Soto-Kanda. Akihabara station.
☏ 03 6252 3263, ⓦ maidreamin.com. Daily
10am–11pm.
Spangly, anime-like maid café,
whose English-speaking staff will
let you know exactly which cute
poses to make, which cute sounds
to mimic and so on. It's all rather
fun, and charged at ¥500 per
person per hour, with an order
from the menu mandatory.

Restaurants

Botan
MAP P.42, POCKET MAP H4
1-15 Kanda-Sudachō. Awajichō station.
☏ 03 3251 0577. Daily (except Sun)
11.30am–9pm.
Chicken *sukiyaki* (a stew-like dish
served in a hotpot) is the order
of the day at this atmospheric
old restaurant, tucked into the
backstreets of Kanda; think around
¥7000 a head.

Go Go Curry
MAP P.42, POCKET MAP J4
1-16-1 Kanda-Sakumachō. Akihabara
station. ☏ 03 5256 5525, ⓦ gogocurry.com.

Daily 9.55am–9.55pm.
No doubt about it, the official
meal of Akihabara regulars is
tonkatsu curry (fried pork cutlet
on rice, smothered in curry
sauce), and this is one of the
heartiest you'll find; plates start
at ¥730.

Hachimaki
MAP P.42, POCKET MAP G5
1-19 Kanda-Jimbōchō. Jimbōchō station.
☏ 03 3291 6222. Daily 11am–9pm.
Dating back to 1931, this tempura
specialist is one of Tokyo's best
time-warp restaurants: there's nary
a sign that you're in the twenty-
first century. Have a crack at their
delectable *tendon*, which gets you
four freshly made tempura on rice
(¥800), or a full set (¥2000).

Toritsune Shizendo
MAP P.42, POCKET MAP H4
5-5-2 Soto-Handa. Suehirochō station.
☏ 03 5818 3566. Daily (except Sun)
1.30am–1.30pm & 5.30–10pm.
Simple place serving some of the
best oyakodon (basically chicken
and egg on rice) around, for the
very fair price of ¥1100.

Ueno and around

Directly north of Akihabara is Ueno, another of Tokyo's teeming mega-neighbourhoods. Around the area's main park, Ueno Kōen, you'll find a host of good museums, as well as a few relics from the vast temple complex at Kan'ei-ji, built on this hilltop in 1624 by the second shogun, Tokugawa Hidetada, to protect his castle's northeast quarter. The prestigious Tokyo National Museum alone could easily fill a day, but there's also the entertaining Museum of Nature and Science, the Museum of Western Art and the endearing Shitamachi Museum, which harks back to Ueno's proletarian past. Much of downtown Ueno, meanwhile, has a rough-and-ready feel, especially around the station and bustling Ameyokochō Market. Further west, there's a more sedate atmosphere in and around the ivory towers of Tokyo University.

Ueno Kōen

MAP P.48, POCKET MAP J2
上野公園, various entrances; information desk by east gate. Ueno station.

Although it's far from being the city's most attractive park, **Ueno Kōen** is a very pleasant place for a stroll, particularly around Shinobazu Pond, whose western banks are lined with ancient cherry trees. At the top of the steps leading up to the park from Ueno station you'll find a bronze statue of **Saigō Takamori**, the great leader of the Restoration army, which helped bring Emperor Meiji to power – his life story was the inspiration for the Tom Cruise movie *The Last Samurai*.

Ueno Zoo

MAP P.48, POCKET MAP H2
上野動物園, 9–83 Ueno Kōen. ☎ 03 3828 5171, ⚓ tokyo-zoo.net. Tues–Sun 9.30am–4pm. ¥600, free for children 12 and under; monorail ¥150.

Considering the fact that **Ueno Zoo** is over a century old, it's less depressing than might be feared; there's plenty of vegetation around, including some magnificent,

corkscrewing lianas. Among the animals here are rare gorillas and pygmy hippos, as well as a couple of pandas, and some macaques who seem to have a whale of a time on the rocky crag they call home; the same cannot be said of the bears and big cats, who tend to pace around small corners of their pens. The east and west parts of the zoo are connected by monorail, though walking is just as pleasant.

Shitamachi Museum

MAP P.48, POCKET MAP H3
下町風俗資料館, 2-1 Ueno Kōen. Ueno or Ueno-Hirokōji stations. ☎ 03 3823 7451, ⚓ www.taitocity.net/taito/shitamachi. Tues–Sun 9.30am–5.30pm. ¥300.

The interesting **Shitamachi Museum** preserves something of the working-class Shitamachi of old; its ground floor is made up of a reconstructed merchant's shophouse and a 1920s tenement row, complete with sweet shop and coppersmith's workroom. The upper floor is devoted to rotating exhibitions focusing on articles of daily life – old photos, toys, advertisements and artisans' tools, with all exhibits donated by local residents.

Tōshō-gū

MAP P.48, POCKET MAP H2

東照宮, 9-88 Ueno. Ueno or Nezu stations. Daily 9am–sunset. ¥200.

A tree-lined avenue marks the approach to Tokugawa Ieyasu's shrine, **Tōshō-gū**. Ieyasu died in 1616 and is buried up north in Nikkō, but this was his main shrine in Tokyo, founded in 1627 and rebuilt on a grander scale in 1651. A path leads round the polychrome halls and into the worship hall, whose faded decorative work contrasts sharply with the burnished black and gold of Ieyasu's shrine room behind.

National Museum of Western Art

MAP P.48, POCKET MAP J2

国立西洋美術館, 7-7 Ueno Kōen. Ueno station. ☏ 03 3828 5131, ⓦ nmwa. go.jp. Tues–Sun 9.30am–5.30pm, Fri until 8pm. ¥500, or more for special exhibitions.

The **National Museum of Western Art** is instantly recognizable from the Rodin statues on the forecourt. The museum, designed by Le Corbusier, was erected in 1959 to house the mostly French Impressionist paintings left to the nation by Kawasaki shipping magnate Matsukata Kōjirō. Since then, works by Rubens, Tintoretto, Max Ernst and Jackson Pollock have broadened the scope of this impressive collection.

National Museum of Nature and Science

MAP P.48, POCKET MAP J2

国立科学博物館, 7-20 Ueno Kōen. Ueno station. ☏ 03 5777 8600, ⓦ www. kahaku.go.jp. Tues–Sun 9am–5pm, Fri until 8pm. ¥620.

The **National Museum of Nature and Science** offers lots of videos and interactive displays, and was recently expanded to include new, slightly fancier, wings on most floors. Six floors of displays cover natural history as well as science and technology. In the "exploration space" on the second floor, pendulums, magnets, mirrors and hand-powered generators provide entertainment for the mainly school-age audience, while down in the basement there's an

Ueno Zoo

aquarium and a dinosaur skeleton. One interesting highlight is on the second floor: sitting amid other stuffed animals, with surprisingly little fanfare, is Hachikō, Japan's canine hero (see page 82). Almost all visitors, even the locals, walk past without a second glance – a rather sad end for the country's most famous hound.

Tokyo National Museum

MAP P.48, POCKET MAP J2

東京国立博物, 13-9 Ueno Kōen. Ueno station. ☏ 03 5405 8686, ⓦ www.tnm. jp. Tues–Sun 9.30am–5pm, though often later. ¥620.

Dominating the northern reaches of Ueno Park is the **Tokyo National Museum**, containing the world's largest collection of Japanese art, plus an extensive collection of eastern antiquities. Displays are rotated every few months from a collection of around 110,000 pieces, and the special

exhibitions are usually worth seeing if you can stand the crowds.

It's best to start with the **Japanese Gallery**, the central building, which presents the sweep of Japanese art from Jōmon-period pottery (pre-fourth century BC) to paintings from the Edo period; look out for theatrical costumes colourful Buddhist mandalas, *ukiyo-e* prints, samurai swords, exquisite lacquerware and even seventeenth-century Christian art from southern Japan.

To the northwest, the splendid **Japanese Archeology Gallery** contains important recent finds; highlights are the chunky, flame-shaped Jōmon pots and a collection of super-heated Sue stoneware, made using a technique introduced from Korea in the fifth century. The upper level hosts special exhibitions – usually very well curated.

In the southwest corner of the compound lurks the sleek **Gallery of**

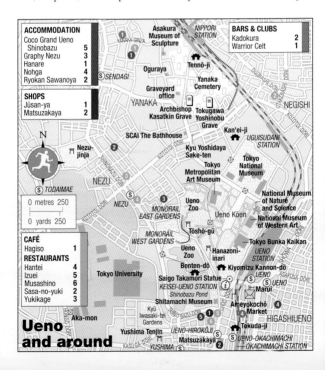

Hōryū-ji Treasures, which contains a selection of priceless artefacts donated over the centuries to the Hōryū-ji in Nara, many dating back as far as the seventh century.

Lastly, the **Asian Gallery** houses a delightful hotchpotch of antiquities, with Javanese textiles and nineteenth-century Indian prints rubbing shoulders with Egyptian mummies (not quite Asian, but evidently close enough) and a wonderful collection of Southeast Asian bronze Buddhas.

Kyū Iwasaki-tei Gardens

MAP P.48, POCKET MAP H3
旧岩崎邸庭園, 1-3-45 Ikenohata. Yushima station. ☎ 03 3823 8340. Daily 9am–5pm. ¥400; tea ¥500.

Off the southeastern corner of Tokyo University, the **Kyū Iwasaki-tei Gardens** date from 1896 and surround an elegant **house**, designed by British architect Josiah Conder, which combines a *café au lait*-painted, Western-style two-storey mansion with a traditional single-storey Japanese residence. The wooden Jacobean- and Moorish-influenced arabesque interiors of the mansion are in fantastic condition, in stark contrast to the severely faded screen paintings of the Japanese section. You can take **tea** in the Japanese section or sit outside and admire the gardens, which also combine Eastern and Western influences.

Nezu-jinja

MAP P.48, POCKET MAP G2
根津神社, 1-28-9 Nezu. Nezu station. Daily 7am–sunset. Free.

The cracking **Nezu-jinja** shrine dates from the early eighteenth century when it was built in honour of the sixth Tokugawa shogun, Ienobu. Ornate and colourfully decorated, it is notable for its corridor of vermilion *torii* (you may have to stoop to get under them) and a hillside bedecked with some three thousand azalea bushes which bloom in a

Yanaka Cemetery

profusion of pinks and reds during late April and early May, attracting throngs of camera-toting visitors. At other times the shrine is serene and peaceful.

Yanaka Cemetery

MAP P.48, POCKET MAP H1
谷中霊園, Nippori station. 24hr. Free.

The Yanaka area is dominated by **Yanaka Cemetery**, one of Tokyo's oldest and largest graveyards. There are various notables who have been laid to rest here, including the last Tokugawa shogun, Yoshinobu, who is buried in a large plot on the southern edge of the cemetery.

SCAI The Bathhouse

MAP P.48, POCKET MAP H2
スカイザバスハウス, 6-1-23 Yanaka. Nippori or Nezu stations. ☎ 03 3821 1144, ⓦ scaithebathhouse.com. Tues–Sat noon–6pm. Free.

A bizarre little contemporary art gallery, **SCAI The Bathhouse** occupies a 200-year-old public bath west of Yanaka Cemetery. It's best known for bringing younger local artists greater international attention, though its own exhibits are often sourced from abroad – this successful East–West interplay resulted in both Anish Kapoor and Julian Opie finding Japanese inspiration.

Shops

Jūsan-ya

MAP P.48, POCKET MAP H3

2-12-21 Ueno. Ueno-Hirokōji station. ☏ 03 3831 3238. Mon–Sat 10am–6.30pm.
Tiny shop across the road from Shinobazu Pond, where a craftsman sits making beautiful boxwood combs – just as successive generations have done since 1736.

Matsuzakaya

MAP P.48, POCKET MAP H3

3-29-5 Ueno. Ueno-Hirokōji station. ☏ 03 3832 1111, ⓦ www.matsuzakaya.co.jp/ueno. Daily 10am–8pm.
This 300-year-old department store is based in Ueno, where its main outlet barely shows its age thanks to an updated look.

Café

Hagiso

MAP P.48, POCKET MAP H1

3-10-25 Yanaka. Sendagi station. ☏ 03 5834 7301, ⓦ hanare.hagiso.jp. Daily 8am–10.30am & noon–9pm.

This black-painted building is the best café in the area by far, with great coffee (from ¥500), a choice of desserts including cheesecake and parfaits, and an artistic atmosphere often enlivened by small exhibitions.

Restaurants

Hantei

MAP P.48, POCKET MAP H2

2-12-15 Nezu. Nezu station. ☏ 03 3828 1440, ⓦ hantei.co.jp. Tues–Sat noon–2.30pm & 5–10pm, Sun 11.30am–2.30pm & 4–9.30pm.
Beautiful restaurant in a three-storey wooden house, doling out *kushiage* (deep-fried meat, fish and vegetables skewered on sticks), six at a time: ¥3000 for the first plate and ¥1500 thereafter, until you say stop.

Izuei

MAP P.48, POCKET MAP H3

2-12-22 Ueno. Ueno station. ☏ 03 3831 0954. Daily 11am–9.30pm.
Fancy eel specialist on the southern fringe of Shinobazu Pond, selling delectable unadon (eel on rice) from ¥3240, or

Matsuzakaya

Hagiso

¥2700 if you're one of the first twenty in for lunch.

Musashino

MAP P.48, POCKET MAP H3
2F 2-8-1 Ueno. Ueno-Hirokōji station. ☏ 03 3831 1672. Daily 11.30am–9pm.
One of Ueno's few remaining old-style restaurants serving thick, melt-in-the-mouth slabs of *tonkatsu*, for which the area was once famed; choose between standard *rōsu* (fatty belly meat) and the leaner *hire* (loin fillet), both costing ¥1000 including soup, rice and pickles.

Sasa-no-yuki

MAP P.48, POCKET MAP J1
2-15-10 Negishi. Uguisudani station. ☏ 03 3873 1145, ⓦ sasanoyuki.com. Tues–Sun 11.30am–9pm.
Three centuries ago, the chef here was said to make tofu like "snow lying on bamboo leaves", and both the name and the quality have survived. Full courses go from ¥5000, or ¥2200 for lunch.

Yukikage

MAP P.48, POCKET MAP H2
2-18-3 Nezu. Nezu station. ☏ 03 5809 0612. Daily (except Mon) 11am–10pm.
This sociable, foreigner-friendly place almost looks more like a bar, thanks to the range of sake and shōchū (they even have local IPA on tap). The noodles themselves are great too (from ¥750).

Bars and clubs

Kadokura

MAP P.48, POCKET MAP J3
6-13-1 Ueno. Ueno station. ☏ 03 3832 5335. Daily 10am–11pm.
Bustling *tachinomiya* that usually gets boisterous – a great place to make new friends over a freezing beer or highball (from ¥400).

Warrior Celt

MAP P.48, POCKET MAP H1
6-9-22 Ueno. Ueno station. ☏ 03 3836 8588, ⓦ warriorcelt.jp. Mon–Thurs 5pm–midnight, Fri & Sat 5pm–5am.
Occasionally wild pub whose regulars are led on by a veritable United Nations of bar staff. Fine range of beers, good food, and a nightly happy hour (5–7pm).

Asakusa and around

Tokyo boasts many wonderful neighbourhoods, but few score as highly as Asakusa for sheer charm. With its historic buildings, craft shops and ryokan, the area wears its tradition gallantly, though it conceals a surprisingly seedy heart – here you'll find vivid reminders of Edo's Shitamachi (see page 53), and the popular culture it spawned. Asakusa is best known as the site of Tokyo's most venerable Buddhist temple, Sensō-ji, whose towering worship hall is filled with a continual throng of petitioners and tourists. Stalls before the temple cater to the crowds, peddling trinkets and keepsakes as they have done for centuries, while all around is the inevitable array of restaurants, drinking places and fast-food stands. This infectious, carnival atmosphere changes abruptly just to the west of the temple, where the Rokku area has long been a byword for sleaze and vice. To the east and across the river is Ryōgoku, a sort of sumo town, and is also home to the absorbing Edo-Tokyo Museum.

Sensō-ji

MAP P.54, POCKET MAP B11
浅草寺, North end of Nakamise-dōri.
Asakusa station. Grounds daily 24hr, main
hall daily 6am–5pm. Free.

The solid red-lacquer Kaminari-mon gate, with its enormous, 670kg paper lantern, marks the southern entrance to **Sensō-ji**. This magnificent temple was

Sensō-ji

founded in the mid-seventh century to enshrine a tiny golden image of the goddess of mercy, which had turned up in the nets of two local fishermen. In front of the temple's main hall, a constant crowd clusters around a large, bronze incense bowl where people waft the pungent smoke over themselves: considered the breath of the gods, and supposed to have curative powers. The hall itself is full of life, with the rattle of coins being tossed into a huge wooden coffer, the swirling plumes of incense smoke and the constant bustle of people coming to pray, buy charms and fortune papers or to attend a service. Three times a day, drums echo through the hall into the courtyard as priests chant sutras beneath the altar's gilded canopy.

Tokyo Skytree

Tokyo Skytree

MAP P.54, POCKET MAP C11
東京スカイツリー, 1-1-2 Oshiage.
Oshiage or Tokyo Skytree stations.
☎ 03 6658 8012, ⓦ tokyo-skytree.jp.
Observation decks daily 8am–10pm. 350m

deck ¥2100/2300 weekdays/weekends;
450m deck ¥1000/1100 extra weekdays/
weekends.

Shitamachi

Although the Tokyo of today is a city made up of umpteen mega-districts, under Tokugawa rule (1603–1867) things were a little different. Edo, as Tokyo was known in those times, was essentially divided by caste: the *daimyō* (feudal lords) and samurai resided in the high city, known as **Yamanote** ("the hand of the mountains"), while merchants, artesans and other elements of the working class lived down in cramped **Shitamachi** ("under-town"), an area which resembled a shantytown, its wooden buildings often going up in flames.

While Yamanote is today best-known as the name of the JR line that encircles central Tokyo, elements of Shitamachi have survived through the intervening centuries, especially in the areas around Ueno and Asakusa (and, indeed, all the way up to Kita-Senju). Some original wooden buildings still stand, and the packed layout of yore is evident in countless meandering alleyways. Many elements of culture now thought of as quintessentially Japanese can trace their lineage back to Shitamachi, too – sumo, kabuki and all manner of arts and crafts started life as subcultures spawned by Shitamachi's unique combination of deprivation and artistic creation.

Kimono rental

At 634m, the **Tokyo Skytree** is the world's second-tallest structure after Dubai's mighty Burj Khalifa (830m). Triangular at the base, its pale-blue, latticed sides gently morph towards a circular shape before hitting the lower observation deck; the second deck is another 100m up, with the super-skinny transmitting antenna protruding another 184m beyond. The views from the observation decks are, predictably, fantastic: giant touch-screen displays show precisely what you're looking at, and also let you see how the view would appear at night (or by day, if you're visiting in the evening). Mount Fuji is, in theory, within visible range, but the unfortunate reality is that mist often blocks the view even in sunny weather, and it's usually only visible a couple of times per month.

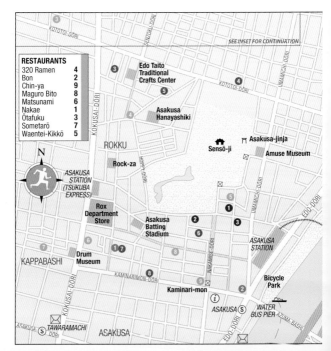

RESTAURANTS

320 Ramen	4
Bon	2
Chin-ya	9
Maguro Bito	8
Matsunami	6
Nakae	1
Ōtafuku	3
Sometarō	7
Waentei-Kikkō	5

Playing dress-up

Asakusa has plenty of shops selling kimono, both new and used, and these can make for fantastic souvenirs. However, if you're not sure that you'll ever need one again, you can make use of the many **kimono rental spots** dotted around the area – there seems to be one on almost every street (there are also a few in Harajuku, Shibuya and other areas). Figure on ¥3000 for the day, and ¥1500 to have your hair done.

Sumida aquarium (Sumida Suizokukan)

MAP P.54, POCKET MAP C11
すみだ水族館, 5F and 6F Tokyo Solamachi West Yard. ☎ 03 5619 1821, ⓦ sumida-aquarium.com. Daily 9am–9pm. ¥2050.

Every major tower in Tokyo seems to have an aquarium attached, and the Skytree is no exception. The **Sumida aquarium** is a pretty good one, though, with a 350,000-litre tank (the largest in Japan) at its centre; clever design of the glass walls mean that you can see the whole tank from almost any angle. Most visitors make a beeline for the seals and penguins, but the jellyfish display is worth tracking down too.

Edo-Tokyo Museum

MAP P.42 & 54, POCKET MAP K4
江戸東京博物館, 1-4-1 Yokoami. Ryōgoku station. ☎ 03 3626 9974, ⓦ edo-tokyo-museum.or.jp. Tues–Fri & Sun 9.30am–5.30pm, Sat 9.30am–7.30pm. ¥600.

Housed in a colossal building (modelled on a *geta*) behind

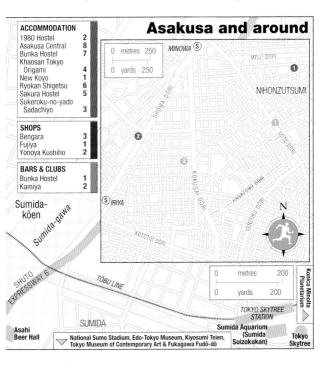

Edo-Tokyo Museum

the Sumo Stadium, the **Edo-Tokyo Museum** tells the history of Tokyo from the days of the Tokugawa shogunate to postwar reconstruction, using life-size replicas, models and holograms, as well as more conventional screen paintings, ancient maps and documents. The museum starts on the sixth floor, where a bridge (a replica of the original Nihombashi) takes you over the roofs of some mock Edo landmarks – a kabuki theatre, *daimyō* residence and Western-style newspaper office – on the main exhibition floor below.

Kiyosumi Teien

MAP P.54, POCKET MAP A12
清澄庭園, 3-9 Kiyosumi. Kiyosumi-shirakawa station. ☎ 03 3641 5892. Daily 9am–5pm. ¥150.

A beautiful Edo-era garden surrounding a large pond, **Kiyosumi Teien** counts as a must-see if you're in the area. Originally the property of a merchant, the gardens were landscaped to within an inch of their life upon their acquisition by a local feudal lord; the stones that you'll see around the grounds come from all over Japan. The gardens are particularly worth visiting in spring for their cherry blossom and azaleas.

Tokyo Museum of Contemporary Art

MAP P.54, POCKET MAP B12
東京都現代美術館, 4-1-1 Miyoshi. ☎ 03 5245 4111, ⓦ mot-art-museum.jp. Daily (except Mon) 10am–6pm. ¥500, plus more for special exhibitions.15min walk north of Kiba station.

A severe glass-and-grey-steel building houses Tokyo's premier modern art venue, the **Tokyo Museum of Contemporary Art**.

Sumo

Japan's national sport, **sumo**, developed out of the divination rites performed at Shintō shrines, and its religious roots are still apparent in the various rituals which form an integral part of a *basho*, or **tournament**. These take place in odd-numbered months; Tokyo's are in January, May and September. Bouts involve two huge wrestlers, each weighing 170 kilos on average and wearing nothing but a hefty loincloth, facing off in a small ring of hard-packed clay. The loser is the first to step outside the rope or touch the ground with any part of the body except the feet – the contest is often over in seconds, but the **pageantry** and ritual make for a wonderfully absorbing spectacle. The top two divisions of wrestlers fight on each afternoon of the fifteen-day-long tournament, and the top-division fighter with the most wins is declared champion; in recent years, champions have been almost exclusively **Mongolian** in origin. Tickets are available from ticket agencies, but the cheapest ones (up in the gods) are only sold on the day (¥2200); these days you'll have to come early to get a ticket, especially on the first and last days of the 15-day tournament.

The vast spaces inside provide the perfect setting for a fine collection of works by various artists from the post-1945 avant-garde through the 1950s abstract revolution to pop art, minimalism and beyond; most are Japanese in origin, but you'll see works from prominent Western artists too (notably Roy Lichtenstein).

Fukagawa Fudō-dō

MAP P.54, POCKET MAP B13
深川不動堂, 1-17-3 Tomioka.
Monzennakachō station. ☎ 03 3641 8288.
Fire rituals 9am, 11am, 1pm, 3pm & 5pm.
Just south of the main Kiyosumi sights, and reached via an unusually blocky *torii*, the **Fukagawa Fudō-dō** is certainly up there with Tokyo's most interesting temples, thanks to its liberal use of fire – rituals involving objects being passed over flames take place at least five times daily, with drums and sutra-chanting providing atmospheric backing tracks. Don't miss the stunning prayer corridor, in which almost 10,000 crystal Buddha statues glow in the dark.

Kiyosumi Teien

Shops

Bengara

MAP P.54, POCKET MAP B11

1-35-6 Asakusa. Asakusa station. ☎ 03 3841 6613. Daily 10am–6pm; closed third Sun of month.

This tiny store is crammed with a wide variety of *noren*, the split curtain seen hanging outside every traditional shop or restaurant. Even if you don't own a shop or restaurant, there'll be somewhere suitable in your own home for one of these.

Fujiya

MAP P.54, POCKET MAP B11

2-2-15 Asakusa. Asakusa station. ☎ 03 3841 2283. Daily (except Thurs) 10am–6pm.

Hand-printed cotton towels (*tenugui*); some end up becoming collectors' items, so choose carefully.

Yonoya Kushiho

MAP P.54, POCKET MAP B11

1-37-10 Asakusa. Asakusa station. ☎ 03 3844 1755. Daily (except Wed) 10.30am–6pm.

Tokyo's finest hand-crafted boxwood combs and hair decorations; much of the wood used here is sourced from forest land south of Kagoshima, and it's reputed to be particularly suitable for hair.

Restaurants

320 Ramen

MAP P.54, POCKET MAP B11

2-15-1 Asakusa, Asakusa station. Daily (except Sat) 10am–7.30pm.

Don't expect any culinary fireworks at this spit-and-sawdust ramen bar, but the bowls – at just ¥320 – are excellent backpacker fare, and they don't taste too bad at all.

Bon

MAP P.54, POCKET MAP K1

1-2-11 Ryusen. Iriya station. ☎ 03 3872 0375, ⓦ fuchabon.co.jp. Mon & Tues, Thurs & Fri noon–1.30pm & 5–7pm, Sat noon–7pm, Sun noon–6pm.

A rare chance to sample *fucha ryōri*, a Zen Buddhist cuisine in which each of the ornately presented vegetable dishes is traditionally served from one large bowl. Reservations essential, with courses starting at ¥5400.

Chin-ya

MAP P.54, POCKET MAP B11

1-3-4 Asakusa. Asakusa station. ☎ 03 3841 0010, ⓦ www.chinya.co.jp. Mon & Wed–Fri noon–3.30pm & 4.30–9.30pm, Sat & Sun 11.30am–9pm.

Founded in 1880, this famous *shabu-shabu* and *sukiyaki* (styles of Japanese hotpots) restaurant offers sets from ¥5500. The place occupies seven whole floors.

Maguro Bito

MAP P.54, POCKET MAP B11

1-21-8 Asakusa. Asakusa station. ☎ 03 3844 8736, ⓦ magurobito.com. Mon–Fri 11.30am–9.30pm, Sat & Sun 11am–10pm.

Once voted this the top *kaiten-zushiya* (revolving sushi restaurant) in Japan, the turnover here is fast, and the decor on the ritzy side. Plates range from ¥170 to ¥530.

Matsunami

MAP P.54, POCKET MAP A11

1-11-6 Asakusa. Asakusa or Tawaramachi stations. ☎ 03 3844 3737, ⓦ matsunami.net. Mon–Sat 11.30am–2pm & 5–11pm, Sun 11.30am–2pm & 5–10pm.

If you want to try some of Japan's melt-in-the-mouth beef, head to this traditional steakhouse, where lunchtime plates start at ¥1800, including a coffee.

Nakae

MAP P.54, POCKET MAP K1

1-9-2 Nihonzutsumi. Minowa station. ☎ 03 3872 5398, ⓦ sakuranabe.com. Tues–Fri 5–10pm, Sat & Sun 11.30am–9pm.

This venerable restaurant specializes in dishes made with horse meat. Their famous hotpots start at ¥3000, but at least consider splashing out ¥8000 on the full meal.

Ōtafuku

MAP P.54, POCKET MAP K2
1-2-6 Hanakawado. Asakusa station.
☎ 03 3871 2521, ⓦ otafuku.ne.jp.
Mon–Fri 5–10pm, Sat & Sun 11am–1pm & 4–8pm.
Customers clamour to sample this restaurant's delicious selection of *oden* boiled in a soy and *dashi* broth. Individual pieces cost ¥130–600; sit at the counter and point at what you want in the bubbling brass vats.

Sometarō

MAP P.54, POCKET MAP A11
2-2-2 Nishi-Asakusa. Tawaramachi station. ☎ 03 3844 9502. Daily noon–10.30pm.
This rambling, wooden restaurant specializing in *okonomiyaki* (¥550–1380). There are English instructions on the menu, and staff are pleased to help with your on-the-table creations.

Waentei-Kikkō

MAP P.54, POCKET MAP B11
2-2-13 Asakusa. Asakusa station. ☎ 03 5828 8833, ⓦ waentei-kikko.com. Daily (except Wed) 11.30am–1.30pm & 5–9.30pm.

A rare chance to see an excellent live performance of the *shamisen* (Japanese lute) in a delightful wooden house. The lunch bentō is beautifully presented *kaiseki*-style food and costs ¥2500; dinner starts at ¥6800.

Bars and clubs

Bunka Hostel

MAP P.54, POCKET MAP B11
1-13-5 Asakusa. Asakusa station. ☎ 03 5806 3444, ⓦ bunkahostel.jp. Daily (except Mon) 6pm–2am.
The lobby of this excellent hostel doubles as a bar, as stylish as any in the area. They've more than thirty varieties of sake on offer, with the type (dry, sweet, strong, etc) explained on the English-language menu.

Kamiya

MAP P.54, POCKET MAP B11
1-1-1 Asakusa. Asakusa station.
☎ 03 3841 5400. Daily (except Tues) 11.30am–10pm.
Established in 1880, this was Tokyo's first Western-style bar. It's famous for its Denki Bran ("electric brandy" – a mix of gin, wine, Curaçao and brandy; ¥270), invented here in 1883.

Kamiya

Bayside Tokyo

So thoroughly urban is Tokyo that it can seem surprising to discover that the city is actually beside the sea. Yet many of the *ukiyo-e* masterpieces of Hokusai and Hiroshige depict waterside scenes around Tokyo Bay, and several of the city's prime attractions are to be found here, not least the vast Tsukiji fish market, whose proposed relocation has been a major controversy of late. Across the bay to the south lies Odaiba, built on vast islands of reclaimed land; its principal sights are a couple of excellent museums and a raucous onsen complex, as well as some of Tokyo's most striking and distinctive architecture.

Wholesale Fish Market

MAP P.61, POCKET MAP B–C18
水産卸売場棟, Shijo-mae monorail; also walkable from Toyosu station.
Ⓦ shijo.metro.tokyo.jp. Daily (except Sun) 5am–5pm; auctions daily (except Sun) 5.30–6.30am. Free.
The three interconnected buildings that constitute Toyosu's **Wholesale Fish Market** are filled with eels from Taiwan, salmon from Santiago and tuna from Tasmania are among the 480 different types of seafood – almost two thousand tonnes of it come under the hammer here daily. Most famed are the tuna, which are auctioned off each day – frozen rock-solid, they look rather like steel torpedoes, and are all labelled with yellow stickers indicating their weight and country of origin.

KidZania Tokyo

MAP P.61, POCKET MAP K9
キッザニア東京, 2-4-9 Toyosu. Toyosu station or monorail. ☎ 0120 924901, Ⓦ www.kidzania.jp. Daily 9am–3pm & 4–9pm. Adults ¥1850, children ¥2950–4800 depending on age and visiting time.
Set inside a giant shopping mall, **KidZania Tokyo** is an imaginative mini theme-park where kids run all the various shops and services. It's designed for children aged 2 to 12, and although everything is in Japanese it's possible for non-Japanese-speaking children to join in the fun.

Panasonic Center Tokyo

MAP P.61, POCKET MAP C19
パナソニックセンター東京, 3-5-1 Ariake. Ariake or Kokusai Tenjijō Seimon monorail stations. ☎ 03 3599 2600, Ⓦ panasonic.com/global. Tues–Sun 10am–6pm. Free; RiSuPia ¥500.
The **Panasonic Center Tokyo** is the main showcase of the mammoth electronics group. Here you can try out the latest Nintendo games on a large-screen plasma display or high-resolution projector, as well as check out the company's technologies of tomorrow. The centre includes the fun "digital network museum" **RiSuPia**, at which you're issued with an electronic tag upon entering; as you learn about science and mathematics from the computer games and simulations within the high-tech display hall, the tag keeps track of how well you're doing.

Wonder Wheel

MAP P.61, POCKET MAP B20
ワンダーウィール, Daily 10am–10pm. ¥1000.

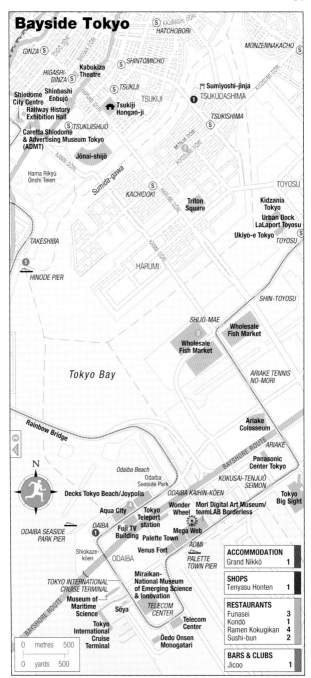

It's hard to miss the **Wonder Wheel**, a candy-coloured, 115m-diameter Ferris wheel, which takes sixteen minutes to make a full circuit. If heights hold no fear then plump for one of the wheel's four fully transparent gondolas, which enable you to see down through the floor; they cost no extra, though you may have to queue.

Mori Digital Art Museum

MAP P.61, POCKET MAP D9
Mon–Fri 10am–7pm, Sat & Sun 10am–9pm, closed 2nd & 4th Tues of month. Ⓦ borderless.teamlab.art. ¥3200.

Odaiba's newest and most fabulous attraction is the **Mori Digital Art Museum**; visitors are encouraged to touch, disrupt or enhance the exhibits, some of which flow between rooms, meaning that the "art" itself continues to morph. As such, it's a little hard to explain what the experience will be like during your own visit – expect things like mirror-filled infinity rooms, "forests" of dangling lamps, projected flowers or giant balloons, and a very, very strange teahouse.

Ōedo Onsen Monogatari

MAP P.61, POCKET MAP B21
大江戸温泉物語, 2-6-3 Aomi. Telecom Center monorail station, or free shuttle buses from Shinagawa, Tokyo and Tokyo Teleport stations. Ⓦ daiba. ooedoonsen.jp. Daily 11am–9am (next day). Mon–Fri ¥2720 (¥2180 after 6pm), Sat & Sun ¥2940 (¥2400 after 6pm), ¥2160 surcharge 1am–6am.

More of a theme park than a bathhouse, the giant **Ōedo Onsen Monogatari** goes in for nostalgic kitsch in a big way. Extra fees are charged for massages, hot sand and stone baths and a separate footbath in which tiny fish nibble the dead skin from your feet – more pleasant than it sounds. Free shuttle buses head here, so if you're planning to hit the onsen

you can save some money on your trip to Odaiba.

Miraikan

MAP P.61, POCKET MAP B20
日本科学未来館, 2-3-6 Aomi. Telecom Center monorail station. ☎ 03 3570 9151, Ⓦ www.miraikan.jst.go.jp. Daily (except Tues) 10am–5pm. ¥620, Dome Theater ¥300.

West of Palette Town is Tokyo's best science museum, the **Miraikan**. Here you can learn about the latest in robot technology, superconductivity (including Maglev trains), space exploration, earthquakes and much more, as well as check out the weather around the world by looking up at a giant sphere covered with one million light-emitting diodes showing the globe as it appears from space that day.

Odaiba beach

MAP P.61, POCKET MAP B19
お台場浜, Daiba monorail station.
On the north side of the island, Odaiba's man-made **beach** – part of **Odaiba Seaside Park** – boasts a fantastic view of the Rainbow Bridge, as well as an unexpected scale copy of the Statue of Liberty. It's a wonderful place to be in the evening, looking at the bridge and twinkly lights beyond, especially if you take off your shoes and dip your feet into the water.

Fuji TV Building

MAP P.61, POCKET MAP B20
富士テレビビル, 2-4-8 Daiba. Daiba monorail. Viewing platform Tues–Sun 10am–6pm. ¥700.

A surreal, sci-fi aura hangs over Tange Kenzō's **Fuji TV Building** – with a huge metal sphere suspended in its middle, it looks as if it's been made from a giant Meccano set. You can head up to the free rooftop "garden" on the seventh floor (just be warned that there's not much greenery), or pay to visit the 25th-floor **viewing platform**.

Restaurants

Funasei

MAPS P.61 & 74, POCKET MAP D16
Kitashinagawa station. ☎ 03 5479 2731,
Ⓦ funasei.com.

Bay cruises, lasting two and a
half hours, run out of Shinagawa
and offer a choice of Japanese-
and Western-style menus, with
unlimited bar access, for around
¥10,800 per person.

Kondō

MAP P.61, POCKET MAP J8
3-12-10 Tsukushima. Tsukishima station.
☎ 03 3533 4555. Mon–Fri 5–10pm, Sat &
Sun noon–10pm.

This is the best *monjayaki*
restaurant in the part of town that
invented this more liquid version of
okonomiyaki. They've a wide range
(¥700–1600); options for the mix
include spicy roe, tuna-corn-cheese,
curry, or chicken and plum paste.

Ramen Kokugikan

MAP P.61, POCKET MAP A19
5F Aqua City, 1-7-1 Daiba. Odaiba Kaihin-
kōen monorail. ☎ 03 3599 4700. Daily
11am–11pm.

Six top ramen chefs from around
Japan square off against each other

in this section of Aqua City's
restaurant floor. A bowl will cost
you from ¥800; the Hakata variety
is well worth trying.

Sushi-bun

MAP P.61, POCKET MAP B18
鮨文, 6-5 Toyosu. Shijō-mae monorail
station. ☎ 03 3541 3860. Daily (except
Sun) 6.30am–2pm.

One of the most *gaijin*-friendly
options among the rows of sushi
stalls within the new Toyosu fish
market. Sets go from ¥3550,
though you won't regret spending
¥1200 more for their top-quality
ten-piece selection, including
creamy *uni* (sea urchin).

Bar/club

Jicoo

MAP P.61, POCKET MAP G9
Hinode station. ☎ 0120 049490,
Ⓦ jicoofloatingbar.com. Daily 8am–11pm.

This futuristic ferry shuttles between
Hinode and Odaiba. To board costs
¥2600; it takes half an hour from
point to point, but you can stay on
as long as you like. Drinks start from
¥700, and there's an illuminated
dancefloor on which to show off
your best John Travolta moves.

Jicoo, floating bar

Akasaka and Roppongi

At one time, Akasaka and Roppongi were pretty much all about nightlife – the former a nocturnal playground for bureaucrats and politicians, the latter an even more boozy place aimed at younger Japanese and *gaijin*. In recent years, with the opening of complexes such as Tokyo Midtown, the emphasis has shifted to daytime activity. Roppongi is styling itself as Tokyo's arts hub, home to the National Art Center, Suntory Museum of Art and Mori Art Museum, the last of which sits atop the area's other mega-development, Roppongi Hills. Both districts have old-established attractions, too, such as Akasaka's premier shrine, Hie-jinja; Zōjō-ji, near Roppongi, once the temple of the Tokugawa clan; and some pretty Japanese gardens. And while Tokyo Tower is no longer the city's most elevated viewing spot, it remains an iconic landmark.

Hie-jinja

MAP P.66, POCKET MAP E7
日枝神社, 2-10-15 Nagatachō.
Akasaka, Akasaka-mitsuke or Tameike-sannō stations. 24hr. Free.

A picturesque avenue of red *torii* lead up the hill to **Hie-jinja**, a Shintō shrine dedicated to the god Ōyamakui-no-kami, who is believed to protect against evil. Hie-jinja's history stretches back to 830 AD, when it was first established on the outskirts of what would become Edo. The shrine's location shifted a couple more times before Shogun Tokugawa Ietsuna placed it here in the seventeenth century as a source of protection for his castle (now the site of the Imperial Palace); the current buildings date from the 1950s.

Toyokawa Inari Tokyo Betsuin

MAP P.66, POCKET MAP E7
豊川稲荷東京別院, 1-4-7
Motoakasaka. Akasaka-mitsuke station.
24hr. Free.

The colourful **Toyokawa Inari Tokyo Betsuin**, also known as Toyokawa Inari, is a combined temple and shrine. Such holy places were much more common across Japan before the Meiji government forcibly separated Shintō and Buddhist places of worship. The temple's compact precincts are decked with red lanterns and banners, while the main hall is guarded by statues of pointy-eared foxes wearing red bibs: messengers of the Shintō god Inari, they are found at all Inari shrines.

Musée Tomo

MAP P.66, POCKET MAP F8
智美術館, 4-1-35 Toranomon.
Roppongi-itchōme, Kamiyachō or Toranomon stations. ☎ 03 5733 5131,
🌐 musee-tomo.or.jp. Daily (except Mon) 11am–6pm. Most exhibitions ¥1000.

Home to the outstanding contemporary Japanese ceramics collection of Tomo Kikuchi, the classy **Musée Tomo** gallery is as elegant as its exhibits – fifty-odd pieces carefully spotlit as objets d'art. Inside is a stunning stairwell with a barley-sugar-like banister and slivers of *washi* paper decorating the walls; from the museum's fancy French café and restaurant, there's a lovely view on to the old home's tranquil garden.

Suntory Museum of Art

MAP P.66, POCKET MAP D8
サントリー美術館, **3F Galleria, Tokyo Midtown. ☏ 03 3470 1073, ☒ suntory. co.jp/sma. Mon & Sun 10am–6pm, Wed–Sat 10am–8pm. Entry price varies by exhibition, usually around ¥1000.**
Landscaped gardens planted with 140 trees nestle behind and along the west side of the Tokyo Midtown complex, where you'll find the **Suntory Museum of Art**. This elegant Kuma Kengo-designed building hosts changing exhibitions of ceramics, lacquerware, paintings and textiles.

21_21 Design Sight

MAP P.66, POCKET MAP D8
9-7-6 Akasaka. ☏ 03 3475 2121, ☒ 2121designsight.jp. Daily 10am–7pm. ¥1100.
Two giant triangular planes of steel, concrete and glass peeking out of a green lawn are part of the **21_21 Design Sight**, a fascinating collaboration between architect Andō Tadao and fashion designer Issey Miyake. The main gallery digs one floor into the ground to provide an elevated, airy space in which to view the various design exhibitions.

National Art Center

MAP P.66, POCKET MAP D8
国立新美術館, **7-22-2 Roppongi. Nogizaka or Roppongi station. ☏ 03 6812 9900, ☒ www.nact.jp. Daily (except Tues) 10am–6pm, Fri 10am–8pm. Entrance fee varies with exhibition.**
A billowing wave of pale green glass ripples across the facade of the stunning **National Art Center**, Japan's largest such museum. Of the twelve exhibition rooms, two are devoted to shows curated by the museum (the centre has no collection of its own); the rest of the rooms are organized by various art associations from across Japan,

with the sum total making for a very eclectic mix.

Nogi-jinja

MAP P.66, POCKET MAP D8
乃木神社, **8-11-27 Akasaka. Nogizaka station. 24hr. Free.**
The small shrine and terraced garden of **Nogi-jinja** honour the Meiji-era **General Nogi Maresuke**, a hero in both the Sino-Japanese and Russo-Japanese wars. When the Emperor Meiji died, Nogi and his wife followed the samurai tradition and committed suicide in his house within the shrine grounds.

Mori Art Museum

MAP P.66, POCKET MAP D9
森美術館, **53F Mori Tower, Roppongi Hills. ☏ 03 6406 6100, ☒ mori.art. museum. Daily 10am–10pm, Tues closes 5pm. ¥1800, including Tokyo City View.**
The "Museum Cone", a glass structure enclosing a swirling staircase, forms the entrance to the **Mori Art Museum**, more than

Mori Art Museum

Akasaka and Roppongi

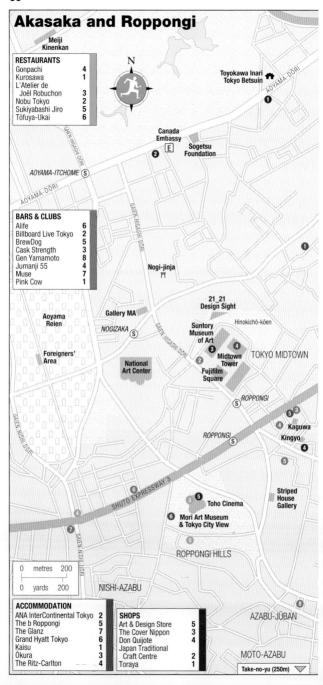

RESTAURANTS

Gonpachi	4
Kurosawa	1
L'Atelier de Joël Robuchon	3
Nobu Tokyo	2
Sukiyabashi Jiro	5
Tōfuya-Ukai	6

BARS & CLUBS

Alife	6
Billboard Live Tokyo	2
BrewDog	5
Cask Strength	3
Gen Yamamoto	8
Jumanji 55	4
Muse	7
Pink Cow	1

ACCOMMODATION

ANA InterContinental Tokyo	2
The b Roppongi	5
The Glanz	7
Grand Hyatt Tokyo	6
Kaisu	1
Ōkura	3
The Ritz-Carlton	4

SHOPS

Art & Design Store	5
The Cover Nippon	3
Don Quijote	4
Japan Traditional Craft Centre	2
Toraya	1

Meiji Kinenkan

Toyokawa Inari Tokyo Betsuin

AOYAMA-DORI

Canada Embassy

Sogetsu Foundation

AOYAMA-ITCHOME

AOYAMA-DORI

GAIEN-HIGASHI-DORI

Nogi-jinja

21_21 Design Sight

Gallery MA

NOGIZAKA

Suntory Museum of Art

Hinokichō-kōen

Aoyama Reien

Foreigners' Area

National Art Center

Midtown Tower

TOKYO MIDTOWN

Fujifilm Square

ROPPONGI

ROPPONGI

Kaguwa

Kingyo

GAIEN-NISHI-DORI

SHUTO EXPRESSWAY 3

Striped House Gallery

Toho Cinema

Mori Art Museum & Tokyo City View

ROPPONGI HILLS

| 0 | metres | 200 |
| 0 | yards | 200 |

NISHI-AZABU

AZABU-JŪBAN

MOTO-AZABU

Take-no-yu (250m)

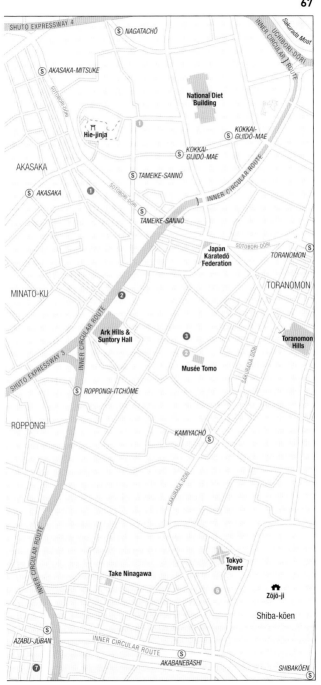

SHUTO EXPRESSWAY 4

Ⓢ NAGATACHŌ

UCHIBORI-DŌRI
INNER CIRCULAR ROUTE
Sakurada Moat

Ⓢ AKASAKA-MITSUKE

SOTOBORI-DŌRI

National Diet
Building

Hie-jinja

①

KOKKAI-
GIJIDŌ-MAE

AKASAKA

KOKKAI-
Ⓢ GIJIDŌ-MAE

Ⓢ AKASAKA

①

Ⓢ TAMEIKE-SANNŌ

SOTOBORI-DŌRI

INNER CIRCULAR ROUTE

Ⓢ
TAMEIKE-SANNŌ

SOTOBORI-DŌRI

Ⓢ
TORANOMON

Japan
Karatedō
Federation

TORANOMON

MINATO-KU

②

Toranomon
Hills

SHUTO EXPRESSWAY 3

INNER CIRCULAR ROUTE

Ark Hills &
Suntory Hall

③

②

SAKURADA-DŌRI

Musée Tomo

Ⓢ ROPPONGI-ITCHŌME

ROPPONGI

KAMIYACHŌ Ⓢ

SAKURADA-DŌRI

INNER CIRCULAR ROUTE

Tokyo
Tower

Take Ninagawa

⑥

Zōjō-ji

Shiba-kōen

Ⓢ
AZABU-JŪBAN

INNER CIRCULAR ROUTE

⑦

Ⓢ
AKABANEBASHI

SHIBAKŌEN Ⓢ

Tokyo City Skyline with view of Tokyo tower

fifty storeys overhead. This large gallery space, which occupies the prime top floors of the Mori Tower, puts on large and adventurous exhibitions, with a particular focus on Asian artists – they're generally extremely well-curated affairs, even down to themed menu items at the on-site café.

Tokyo City View

MAP P.66, POCKET MAP D9
東京シティビュー, 54F Mori Tower, Roppongi Hills. Ⓦ tcv.roppongihills.com. Daily 9am–1am, last entry midnight. ¥1800, including Mori Art Museum; Skydeck ¥500 extra.

In the same tower as the Mori Art Museum, one floor up, the **Tokyo City View** observation deck is one of the best viewpoints in the city. If the weather is fine, it's possible to get out on to the rooftop **Skydeck** for an alfresco view that's particularly enchanting during and after sunset.

Tokyo Tower

MAP P.66, POCKET MAP F9
東京タワー, 4-2-8 Shiba-kōen.

Akabanebashi or Kamiyachō stations. ☏ 03 3433 5111, Ⓦ tokyotower.co.jp. Daily 9am–11pm. Main observatory ¥900, top observatory ¥1900 extra.

You can't miss the distinctive, red-and-white **Tokyo Tower**, a 333m-high replica of the Eiffel Tower. Though it's no longer the city's highest viewpoint, there are good views of Tokyo Bay from the top observation deck, 250m up.

Take-no-yu

MAP P.66, POCKET MAP E9
竹の湯, 1-15-12 Minami-Azabu. Azabu-Jūban station. Tues–Thurs, Sat & Sun 3.30–11.30pm. ¥460.

A short walk south of Azabu-Jūban, the **Take-no-yu** baths are somewhat different to most other Tokyo establishments for one major reason: the water in these parts comes out brown, and is so prized for its medical properties that locals pay to take it away by the litre. The experience of bathing here is a little like being steeped in tea – or being a dirty plate in a sink full of dirty dishwater.

Shops

Art & Design Store

MAP P.66, POCKET MAP D9

3F Roppongi Hills West Walk, 6-10-1 Roppongi. Roppongi station. ☏ 03 6406 6654. Daily 11am–9pm.

A wonderful store near the entrance to Roppongi Hills' City View. The selection is ever-changing, but often features products from some of Japan's most famous contemporary designers.

The Cover Nippon

MAP P.66, POCKET MAP D8

3F Galleria, Tokyo Midtown, 9-7-3 Akasaka. Roppongi station. ☏ 03 5413 0658, ⓦ thecovernippon.jp. Daily 11am–9pm.

Interesting shop with a fantastic selection of Japanese designer goods made by small, quality manufacturers – everything from cotton fabric and furniture to lacquerware.

Don Quijote

MAP P.66, POCKET MAP E8

3-14-10 Roppongi. Roppongi station. ☏ 03 578 6811, ⓦ donki.com. Daily 24hr.

Fancy some sushi-print socks? A mind-boggling array of stuff is piled high and sold cheap here – everything from liquor to sex toys, as well as gadgets galore. A national institution, it's worth visiting just for the gawp factor. Several branches around the city.

Japan Traditional Craft Centre

MAP P.66, POCKET MAP D7

8-1-22 Akasaka. Aoyama-itchōme station. ☏ 03 5785 1001, ⓦ kougeihin.jp. Daily 10am–7pm.

This centre showcases the works of craft associations across the nation – everything from finely crafted chopsticks to elegant lacquerware and metalwork. Great stuff, but not cheap by any means.

Toraya

MAP P.66, POCKET MAP E7

4-9-22 Akasaka. Akasaka-Mitsuke station. ☏ 03 3408 4121, ⓦ toraya-group. co.jp. Mon–Fri 11am–7pm, Sat & Sun 11am–5.30pm.

Makers of *wagashi* (traditional confectionery, often used in tea ceremonies) for the imperial family; sample them, along with green tea, in the upstairs café of this lovingly redesigned building, a symphony in pine.

Restaurants

Gonpachi

MAP P.66, POCKET MAP D9

1-13-11 Nishi-Azabu. Roppongi station. ☏ 03 5771 0170, ⓦ gonpachi.jp. Daily 11.30am–3.30am.

A faux-Edo-period storehouse selling reasonably priced soba (from ¥800) and grilled items (¥270–500) on the ground and second floors, and sushi on the third floor. It's easy to see how the place inspired the climactic scenes of Quentin Tarantino's *Kill Bill Vol. 1*.

Kurosawa

MAP P.66, POCKET MAP F7

2-7-9 Nagatachō. Tameike-sannō station. ☏ 03 3580 9638, ⓦ 9638.net/nagata. Mon–Fri 11.30am–3pm & 5–10pm, Sat noon–9pm.

The design of this atmospheric restaurant was inspired by Akira Kurosawa movie sets, and a meal here is a superb experience. Given the quality, the prices in the downstairs soba section (bowls from under ¥800) are a real steal.

L'Atelier de Joël Robuchon

MAP P.66, POCKET MAP D9

2F Roppongi Hills Hillside, 6-10-1 Roppongi. Roppongi station. ☏ 03 5772 7500, ⓦ robuchon.jp. Daily 11.30am–2.30pm & 6–10pm.

Tokyo outpost of the French master chef, offering tasting menus starting at ¥3520 for lunch, ¥5720 for dinner. Seats at the long counter face the open kitchen, where chefs create mini-masterpieces.

Nobu Tokyo

MAP P.66, POCKET MAP F8
4-1-28 Toranomon. Kamiyachō station.
☎ 03 5733 0070, ⓦ noburestaurants.com.
Mon–Fri 11.30am–2pm & 6–10.30pm, Sat
& Sun 6–10.30pm.

There's a dramatic Japanese-style
design at this restaurant, where you
can sample the famous black-cod
dinner (Robert de Niro's favourite)
for around ¥5550.

Sukiyabashi Jiro

MAP P.66, POCKET MAP D9
3F Ark Mori Building, 6-12-2 Roppongi.
Roppongi station. ☎ 03 5413 6626,
ⓦ sushi-jiro.jp. Daily (except Wed)
11.30am–2pm & 5.30–9pm.

You may have heard of Jiro
Dreams of Sushi, but people also
dream about getting a seat at
Jiro's restaurant; for the next best
thing, head to his son's place. It's a
pricey ¥22,000 for lunch, ¥30,000
for dinner.

Tōfuya-Ukai

MAP P.66, POCKET MAP F9
4-4-13 Shiba-kōen. Akabanebashi station.
☎ 03 3436 1028, ⓦ ukai.co.jp. Daily
11am–10pm.

At the foot of Tokyo Tower,
this stunning re-creation of
an Edo-era mansion serves
unforgettable tofu-based *kaiseki*-
style cuisine. Book well ahead;
set meals only, with lunch from
¥5940 on weekdays, and dinner
from ¥10,800.

Bars and clubs

Alife

MAP P.66, POCKET MAP D9
1-7-2 Nishi-Azabu. Roppongi station. ☎ 03
5785 2531, ⓦ e-alife.net.

Famed club whose second-floor
lounge area is a good place to chill
out after you've worked up a sweat
to the house and techno being
spun on the large dancefloor
below. Events most nights
except Sun.

Billboard Live Tokyo

MAP P.66, POCKET MAP D8
4F Tokyo Midtown 9-7-4 Akasaka.
Roppongi station. ☎ 03 3405 1133,
ⓦ billboard-live.com.

A relatively intimate space at which
everyone on the three levels gets a

Gonpachi Nishi-Azabu

great view of the stage. Acts can be anything from jazz to bossa nova (Sergio Mendes has performed here a few times), and R&B to funk. Events most nights.

BrewDog

MAP P.66, POCKET MAP E8
5-3-2 Roppongi. Roppongi station. ☎ 03 6447 4160, Ⓦ brewdogbar.jp. Mon–Fri 5pm–midnight, Sat & Sun 3pm–midnight.
Craft beer has undergone a second wave in Japan, and this is your best bet in the Roppongi area, with their own five brews forming part of a boozy constellation of 20 beers on tap, plus 60 bottled varieties (from ¥700).

Cask Strength

MAP P.66, POCKET MAP E8
B1 3-9-11 Roppongi. Roppongi station. ☎ 03 6432 9772, Ⓦ cask-s.com. Daily 6pm–late.
Attractive basement venue with one of Tokyo's best selections of whisky, including some rare Japanese choices – those with a nose for Karuizawa or Yamazaki Single Malt will be in paradise.

Gen Yamamoto

MAP P.66, POCKET MAP E9
1-6-4 Azabu-jūban. Azabu-jūban station. ☎ 03 6434 0652, Ⓦ genyamamoto.jp. Tues–Sat 3–11pm.
Small, secretive bar serving some of the best cocktails in the city, often made with fresh fruits and veggies sourced from across the land (and all by "feel", rather than by measure).

Jumanji 55

MAP P.66, POCKET MAP E8
3-10-5 Roppongi. Roppongi station. ☎ 03 5410 5455, Ⓦ jumanji55.com. Open most nights.
Aptly, considering its name, this popular pick-up spot can be a bit of a zoo: with the ¥1000 early-entry fee often including a couple of drinks, there's essentially no entry charge, meaning that on weekends there's barely any wiggle-room.

Jessie J performs at Billboard Live Tokyo

Muse

MAP P.66, POCKET MAP D9
4-1-1 Nishi-Azabu. Roppongi station. ☎ 03 5467 1188, Ⓦ muse-web.com. Closed Mon.
Imaginatively designed club with lots of interesting little rooms to explore or canoodle in. The dancefloor at the back gets packed at weekends (there's room for 1200 people, in theory), when they mostly play r'n'b. Free entry weekdays, weekends ¥3000; women usually go free.

Pink Cow

MAP P.66, POCKET MAP E7
2-7-6 Akasaka. Tameike-sanno station. ☎ 03 6441 2998, Ⓦ thepinkcow.com. Daily 5pm–late.
There's always something interesting going on – book readings, art classes, comedy improv nights – at this funky haven for local artists and writers. They have a good range of imported wines, and tasty Tex-Mex-style food.

Ebisu and the south

The area immediately to the south of Shibuya has, of late, become one of the most fashionable in the city – a maze of chic cafés, tiny clothing boutiques, and lunchtime specials of foreign and fusion cuisine. Like Shibuya, Ebisu is best visited at night, when its many bars and restaurants are at their liveliest. The district is also home to the excellent Tokyo Photographic Art Museum. Head uphill to the west of Ebisu and you'll hit Daikanyama, one of Tokyo's most upscale districts and a great place to chill out at a pavement café or browse boutiques. Dip downhill again to explore a rather more down-to-earth version of the same in Nakameguro, whose cherry tree-lined river banks are prime strolling territory, especially during sakura season.

Tokyo Photographic Art Museum

MAP P.74, POCKET MAP C15

東京都写真美術館, **Yebisu Garden Place.** ☎ 03 3280 0031, ⓦ topmuseum. jp. Tues–Sun 10am–6pm, Thurs & Fri until 8pm. Admission charges vary.

The best sight in the Ebisu area is the **Tokyo Photographic Art Museum**, which hosts excellent exhibitions by major Japanese and Western photographers. There are three full floors of exhibitions (two above ground, one below), with a café on the entrance floor; exhibitions can last anything from two weeks to three months, but there's usually a good spread of themes at any one time.

Hillside Terrace

MAP P.74, POCKET MAP B14

Off Kyū-yamate-dōri. Daikanyama station. ⓦ hillsideterrace.com.

Daikanyama's contemporary style has been defined by the **Hillside Terrace** shopping and dining complex, designed by Maki Fumihiko, recipient of the 1993 Pritzker Prize for architecture. The various stages of Hillside Terrace were developed over nearly a quarter-century, its courtyards and vistas paying homage to ancient Japanese and Buddhist concepts of space. Poke around and you'll find plenty of appealing boutiques and ritzy restaurants and cafés, as well as the fascinatingly designed Tsutaya bookstore.

Tokyo Metropolitan Teien Art Museum

MAP P.74, POCKET MAP D15

東京都庭園美術館, **5-21-9 Shirokanedai. Meguro or Shirokanedai stations.** ☎ 03 3443 0201, ⓦ www. teien-art-museum.ne.jp. Museum daily 10am–6pm, closed second & fourth Wed of the month. Entry varies by exhibitions, usually ¥1000. Garden daily 10am–9pm. Entry included with museum ticket, otherwise ¥200.

The Art Deco building housing the elegant **Tokyo Metropolitan Teien Art Museum** is the former home of Prince Asaka Yasuhiko, Emperor Hirohito's uncle, who lived in Paris for three years during the 1920s, where he developed a taste for the European style. It's worth popping in to admire the gorgeous interior decoration (particularly in the octagonal study room upstairs) and tranquil surrounding Japanese gardens; the exhibitions themselves tend to be curated along similarly genteel lines.

National Park for Nature Study

MAP P.74, POCKET MAP C–D15
自然教育園, 5-21-5 Shirokanedai. Meguro or Shirokanedai station. ⓦ www. ins.kahaku.go.jp. Tues–Sun 9am–4.30pm, May–Aug until 5pm. ¥310.

The spacious **National Park for Nature Study** is a worthy attempt to preserve the original natural features of the countryside before Edo was settled and developed into Tokyo. Among the eight thousand trees in the park are some that have been growing for five hundred years, while frogs can be heard croaking amid the grass beside the marshy ponds. The whole place is a bird-spotter's paradise, and it's also one of the few areas in Tokyo where you can really escape the crowds.

Happōen

MAP P.74, POCKET MAP D15
八芳園, 1-1-1 Shirokanedai. Shirokanedai station. Garden Daily 10am–5pm. Free. Teahouse Daily 11am–5pm. ¥800.

Shirokanedai subway station is the handiest jumping-off point for the lovely **Happōen**. The garden's name means "beautiful from any

Hillside Terrace

angle" and, despite the addition of a modern wedding hall on one side, this is still true. Take a turn through its twisting pathways and you'll pass two bonsai trees, each more than a hundred years old, a stone lantern said to have been carved eight hundred years ago by the Heike warrior Taira-no Munekiyo, and a central pond. Nestling amid the trees is the delightful **teahouse**, where ladies in kimono will serve you *matcha* and *okashi*.

Real-life Mario Kart

While walking around certain parts of Tokyo, you may well see foreigners dressed as superheroes dashing around the city streets in tiny go-karts. This is no marketing stunt, but an activity that you can actually take part in yourself; though inspired by the Mario Kart video game, pressure from Nintendo meant that the game character costumes are no longer on offer. The **Street Kart** team (ⓣ 03 6712 8275, ⓦ kart.st) run three separate courses from their office in Shinagawa; all of them take in Tokyo Tower and Roppongi, with Shibuya and Odaiba also options, and prices start at ¥10,000 (reduced to ¥8500 if you give a positive social media review immediately after your ride). You'll need to be in possession of a foreign or international driving licence, and unlike in the game, you only have one life.

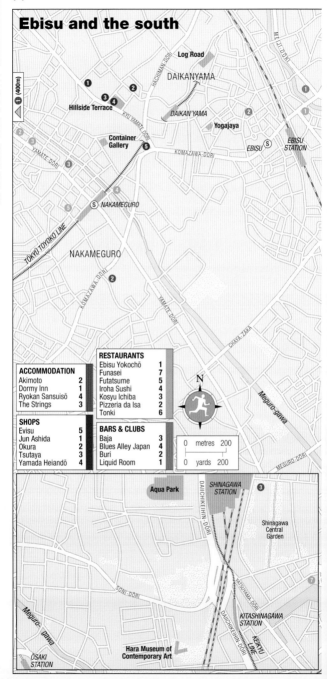

Ebisu and the south

Log Road

DAIKANYAMA

Hillside Terrace

DAIKAN'YAMA

Yogajaya

Container Gallery

KOMAZAWA-DORI

EBISU ⓢ

EBISU STATION

MEIJI-DORI

HACHIMAN-DORI

KYU-YAMATE-DORI

YAMATE-DORI

ⓢ NAKAMEGURO

TŌKYU TŌYOKO LINE

NAKAMEGURO

KOMAZAWA-DORI

YAMATE-DORI

CHAYA-ZAKA

Meguro-gawa

N

ACCOMMODATION	
Akimoto	2
Dormy Inn	1
Ryokan Sansuisō	4
The Strings	3

SHOPS	
Evisu	5
Jun Ashida	1
Okura	2
Tsutaya	3
Yamada Heiandō	4

RESTAURANTS	
Ebisu Yokochō	1
Funasei	7
Futatsume	5
Iroha Sushi	4
Kosyu Ichiba	3
Pizzeria da Isa	2
Tonki	6

BARS & CLUBS	
Baja	3
Blues Alley Japan	4
Buri	2
Liquid Room	1

0 metres 200
0 yards 200

Aqua Park

SHINAGAWA STATION

DAIICHIKEHIN-DORI

Shinagawa Central Garden

SŌNI-DŌRI

MITSUYAMA-DŌRI

KITASHINAGAWA STATION

DAIICHIKEHIN-DORI

KEIKYU LINE

Meguro-gawa

Hara Museum of Contemporary Art

ŌSAKI STATION

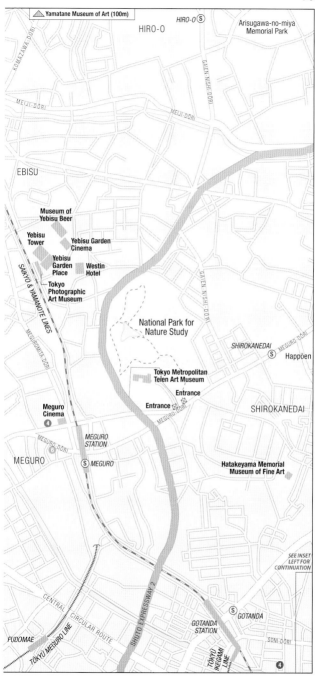

▲ Yamatane Museum of Art (100m)

HIRO-O Ⓢ

HIRO-O

Arisugawa-no-miya
Memorial Park

KOMAZAWA-DORI

GAIEN NISHI-DORI

MEIJI-DORI

MEIJI-DORI

EBISU

Museum of
Yebisu Beer

Yebisu
Tower

Yebisu Garden
Cinema

Yebisu
Garden
Place

Westin
Hotel

Tokyo
Photographic
Art Museum

SAIKYO & YAMANOTE LINES

MEGUROGAWA-DORI

National Park for
Nature Study

GAIEN NISHI-DORI

MEGURO-DORI

SHIROKANEDAI Ⓢ

Happōen

Tokyo Metropolitan
Teien Art Museum

Entrance

Entrance

SHIROKANEDAI

Meguro
Cinema

④

MEGURO-DORI

⑥

MEGURO
STATION

MEGURO-DORI

MEGURO

Ⓢ MEGURO

Hatakeyama Memorial
Museum of Fine Art

SEE INSET
LEFT FOR
CONTINUATION

CENTRAL

CIRCULAR ROUTE

SHUTO EXPRESSWAY 2

Ⓢ GOTANDA

GOTANDA
STATION

SONI-DORI

FUDOMAE

TOKYO MEGURO LINE

TOKYO
IKEGAMI
LINE

④

Shops

Evisu

MAP P.74, POCKET MAP B14

1-1-5 Kami-Meguro. Nakameguro station. ☎ 03 3710 1999, ⓦ evisu.com. Daily noon–8pm.

Main branch of the ultra-trendy – and ultra-pricey – Japanese jeans designer. Stock up here on shirts, T-shirts, sweatshirts and a full range of accessories.

Jun Ashida

MAP P.74, POCKET MAP A14

17-16 Sarugakuchō. Daikanyama station. ☎ 03 3462 5811, ⓦ jun-ashida.co.jp. Daily 11am–7pm.

The headquarters of Jun Ashida, one of Japan's top designers of womenswear, as well as his daughter Tae, who recently achieved fame by becoming the first ever designer of luxury spacewear.

Okura

MAP P.74, POCKET MAP B14

20-11 Sarugaku-chō. ☎ 03 3461 8511. Daily 11am–8pm.

Daikanyama station. Youthful boutique specializing in indigo-dyed traditional and contemporary

Tsutaya bookshop, Daikanyama

Japanese fashions, from jeans and T-shirts to kimono and *tabi* socks. No English sign – look for a low, wooden-style building, usually with some form of indigo fabric hanging outside.

Tsutaya

MAP P.74, POCKET MAP A14

17-5 Sarugaku-chō. Daikanyama station. ☎ 03 3770 2525, ⓦ tsite.jp. Daily 7am–2am.

The design of this bookshop scooped a number of awards. Filled all day, every day with a preening young crowd, it's now the fulcrum of the whole Daikanyama area.

Yamada Heiandō

MAP P.74, POCKET MAP B14

2F Hillside Terrace, 18-12 Sarugaku-chō. Daikanyama station. ☎ 03 3464 5541, ⓦ heiando.com. Mon–Sat 10.30am–7pm, Sun 10.30am–6.30pm.

Hunt down this store for lacquerware – both traditional and contemporary – found on tables no less distinguished than those of the imperial household and Japan's embassies.

Restaurants

Ebisu Yokochō

MAP P.74, POCKET MAP C14

Ebisu, Minato-ku. Ebisu station. Daily 5pm–late.

Not a restaurant, but a whole clutch of them, crammed into a hugely atmospheric covered arcade east of Ebisu station. Come in the evening and take your pick – there's a curry stand, several noodle joints, places specializing in seafood, and even a miniature karaoke bar.

Futatsume

MAP P.74, POCKET MAP A15

3-9-5 Kami-Meguro. Nakameguro station. ☎ 03 3712 2022. Mon–Sat 6pm–3am. Grand little *kushiage* (deep-fried sticks) place, selling skewered

snacks from just ¥100; choices
include breaded camembert,
shiitake and salmon, and they're all
best washed down with a gigantic
highball (¥980).

Iroha Sushi

MAP P.74, POCKET MAP B15
1-5-13 Kami-Meguro. Nakameguro station.
☎ 03 5722 3560, ⓦ irohasushi.com. Daily
11.30am–2.30pm & 5–10.30pm.
Relaxed sushi den that's the
diametric opposite of most diners
in this fancy part of town – you
won't see any hipsters or boho-
types here, just salary-folk and
older locals. Every single piece is
freshly made, yet hearty lunch sets
go from just ¥680.

Kosyu Ichiba

MAP P.74, POCKET MAP A14
1-29-12 Aobadai. Nakameguro station.
☎ 03 3760 7147. Daily 11am–2am.
This chain sells fantastic *tantan-
men* (ramen with a spicy, oily sauce
and minced pork; ¥920), and their
delectable *gyōza* (¥330) aren't far
off. The attractive Nakameguro
branch basically does the simple
things really, really well.

Pizzeria da Isa

MAP P.74, POCKET MAP A14
1-28-9 Aobadai. Nakameguro station. ☎ 03
5768 3739, ⓦ da-isa.jp. Daily (except Mon)
11.30am–2pm & 5.30–11pm.
The Japanese head chef at this
authentically Italian-style pizzeria
scooped a clutch of awards in
Napoli. Pizzas go from ¥1500,
though note that every diner needs
to order one dish and a drink.

Tonki

MAP P.74, POCKET MAP C16
1-1-2 Shimo-Meguro. Meguro station.
☎ 03 3491 9928. Daily (except Tues)
4–10.45pm.
This minimalist, sharp-looking
restaurant is the most famous place
in town for *tonkatsu*. Sets cost from
¥1900, cutlet alone ¥1300; you'll
have to choose between *hire* (fillet)
and *rōsu* (sirloin).

Bars and clubs

Baja

MAP P.74, POCKET MAP A14
1-16-12 Kami-Meguro. Nakameguro
station. Daily 5pm–5am.
Seemingly decorated with
everything the owner could find
in his garage, this is one of the
most entertaining bars in the
Nakameguro area, with a good
mix of foreigners and oddball
Japanese. Drinks (including
cocktails) cost ¥500; and they
also whip up yummy tacos – a
real winner.

Blues Alley Japan

MAP P.74, POCKET MAP C16
B1F Hotel Leon, 1-3-14 Meguro.
Meguro station. ☎ 03 5740 6041,
ⓦ bluesalley.co.jp.
This offshoot of the Washington
DC blues and jazz club occupies
a small basement space near
the station. Apart from blues,
you can expect to hear jazz,
soul and various Latin sounds.
Ticket prices average ¥4500.
Performances usually daily 6pm
& 7.30pm.

Buri

MAP P.74, POCKET MAP B14
1-14-1 Ebisu-nishi. Ebisu station. ☎ 03
3496 7744. Daily 3pm–midnight.
The fifty-strong range of chilled
"one-cup sake" (a sealed glass,
the size of a small can, filled with
sake that you just pull the top off;
¥800) is the speciality at this trendy
tachinomiya that's one of the best
in town.

Liquid Room

MAP P.74, POCKET MAP C14
3-16-6 Higashi. Ebisu station. ☎ 03 5464
0800, ⓦ liquidroom.net.
Live-music venue hosting some
pretty prominent bands; they also
throw DJ events from time to
time in their *Liquid Loft* space.
Tickets ¥2800–5800. Events
most nights.

Harajuku and Shibuya

If it's "wacky" Japan you're after, Harajuku should be neighbourhood number one on your list – indeed, in terms of human traffic, there can be few more fascinating districts on the whole planet. Much of Tokyo's youth culture starts here, on streets which often resemble densely populated catwalks, complete with zany clothing, hairstyles and accessories; in the surrounding soup of quirky boutiques and cafés, you'll be able to kit yourself out and dine in much the same manner as the local fashionistas. Shibuya, just south of Harajuku, is almost absurdly busy – a neon-drenched, *kanji*-splattered, high-rise jungle second only to Shinjuku for sheer eye-popping madness. East of Harajuku, those with gilt-edged credit cards will feel more at home among the antique shops of Aoyama and the big brand boutiques along Omotesandō, the area's key tree-lined boulevard, often referred to as Tokyo's Champs-Elysées.

Meiji-jingū

MAP P.80, POCKET MAP C7

明治神宮, ⓦ meijijingu.or.jp. Daily sunrise–sunset. Free.

Covering parts of both Aoyama and Harajuku are the grounds of **Meiji-jingū**, Tokyo's premier Shintō shrine, a memorial to

Meiji-jingū

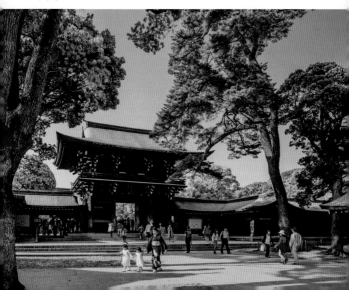

Harajuku style

Swing by the Harajuku station area on a weekend and you'll see crowds of youngsters, mainly female, dressed up to the nines in a series of bizarre costumes; the epicentre is Jingū-bashi, a small bridge heading towards Meiji-Jingū from Harajuku station. There are several distinct styles to look out for, including **Cosplay** (which involves dressing up as an anime, manga or game character), **Gothic Lolita** (a mix of the gothic and the girlie), **Visual Kei** (usually involving heavy make-up and out-there hairstyles), **Decora** (a bright, flamboyant style often featuring myriad toys, pieces of plastic jewellery and other accessories), and **Kawaii** (which usually involves clothing more appropriate to children).

Emperor Meiji and his empress Shōken. Together with the neighbouring shrines to General Nogi and Admiral Tōgō, Meiji-jingū was created as a symbol of imperial power and Japanese racial superiority.

The **Inner Garden**, beside Harajuku station, includes the emperor's shrine, the empress's iris gardens, the Treasure House and extensive wooded grounds. The best approach to the Inner Garden is through the southern gate next to Jingū-bashi, the bridge that crosses over from Harajuku's toytown-like station, complete with mock-Tudor clock tower. From the gateway, a wide gravel path runs through densely forested grounds to the 12m-high **Ō-torii**, the largest Myōjin-style gate in Japan, made from 1500-year-old Taiwanese cypress pine trees.

Signed paths make it simple to push on a little further to the picturesque **Jingū Naien** garden. From here, the gravel path turns right and passes through a second wooden *torii*, **Kita-mon** (north gate), leading to the impressive **Honden** (central hall). With their Japanese cypress wood and green copper roofs, the Honden and its surrounding buildings are a fine example of how Shintō architecture can blend seamlessly with nature.

Ōta Memorial Museum of Art

MAP P.80, POCKET MAP B8
太田記念美術館, **1-10-10 Jingūmae. Harajuku or Meiji-jingumae stations. ⓣ 03 3403 0880, ⓦ ukiyoe-ota-muse.jp. Daily (except Mon) 10.30am–5.30pm. Usually ¥700 for regular exhibitions, ¥1000 for special exhibitions.**

Just off Omotesandō, behind the trendy boutique complex **Laforet**, is the excellent **Ōta Memorial Museum of Art**. Put on slippers to wander through the small galleries on two levels, which feature *ukiyo-e* paintings and prints from the private collection of the late Ōta Seizō, an insurance tycoon. The art displayed comes from a collection of twelve thousand pieces, including masterpieces by Utamaro, Hokusai and Hiroshige.

Okamoto Tarō Memorial Museum

MAP P.80, POCKET MAP C9
岡本太郎記念館, **6-1-19 Minami-aoyama. Omotesandō station. ⓦ taro-okamoto.or.jp. Daily (except Tues) 10am–6pm (final admission 5.30pm). ¥620.**

The quirky **Okamoto Tarō Memorial Museum** once functioned as the studio of the avant-garde artist; it now houses examples of his intriguing, often whimsical work, as well as a pleasant café.

Harajuku and Shibuya

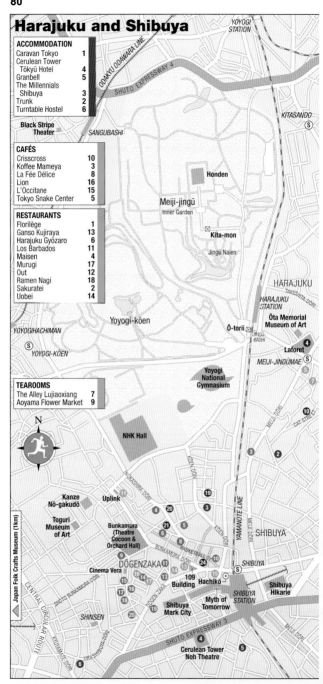

ACCOMMODATION

Caravan Tokyo	1
Cerulean Tower Tōkyū Hotel	4
Granbell	5
The Millennials Shibuya	3
Trunk	2
Turntable Hostel	6

CAFÉS

Crisscross	10
Koffee Mameya	3
La Fée Délice	8
Lion	16
L'Occitane	15
Tokyo Snake Center	5

RESTAURANTS

Florilège	1
Ganso Kujiraya	13
Harajuku Gyōzaro	6
Los Barbados	11
Maisen	4
Murugi	17
Out	12
Ramen Nagi	18
Sakuratei	2
Uobei	14

TEAROOMS

The Alley Lujiaoxiang	7
Aoyama Flower Market	9

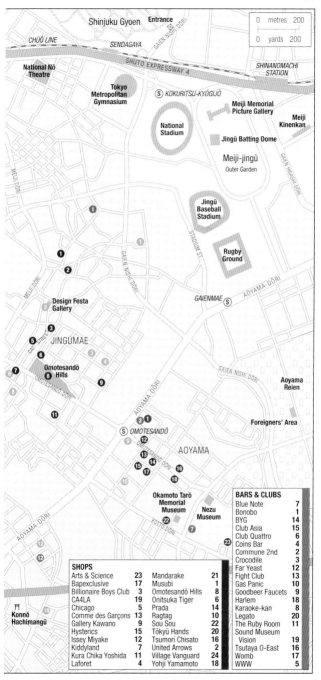

SHOPS

Arts & Science	23
Bapexclusive	17
Billionaire Boys Club	3
CA4LA	19
Chicago	5
Comme des Garçons	13
Gallery Kawano	7
Hysterics	15
Issey Miyake	12
Kiddyland	7
Kura Chika Yoshida	11
Laforet	4
Mandarake	21
Musubi	1
Omotesandō Hills	8
Onitsuka Tiger	6
Prada	14
Ragtag	10
Sou Sou	22
Tōkyū Hands	20
Tsumori Chisato	16
United Arrows	2
Village Vanguard	24
Yohji Yamamoto	18

BARS & CLUBS

Blue Note	7
Bonobo	1
BYG	14
Club Asia	15
Club Quattro	6
Coins Bar	4
Commune 2nd	2
Crocodile	3
Far Yeast	12
Fight Club	13
Gas Panic	10
Goodbeer Faucets	9
Harlem	18
Karaoke-kan	8
Legato	20
The Ruby Room	11
Sound Museum Vision	19
Tsutaya O-East	16
Womb	17
WWW	5

Hachikō

A statue outside Shibuya station marks the waiting spot of **Hachikō** (1923–35), an Akita dog who would come to greet his master every day as he returned home from work – a practice that continued for almost a decade after the professor's death, with the dog arriving on time every day to greet the train. Locals were so touched by Hachikō's devotion that a **bronze statue** was cast of the dog. During World War II, the original Hachikō statue was melted down for weapons, but a replacement was reinstated beside the station in 1948 – it remains one of Tokyo's most famous rendezvous spots. You can see the real Hachikō in the National Science Museum, where he lives on in stuffed form (see page 47).

Nezu Museum

MAP P.80, POCKET MAP C8

根津美術館, 6-5-1 Minami-aoyama. Omotesandō or Nogizaka stations. ☎ 03 3400 2536, ⓦ www.nezu-muse.or.jp. Daily (except Mon) 10am–5pm. ¥1100.

The prestigious **Nezu Museum** sits at the far eastern end of Omotesandō, in an elegant building designed by Kengo Kuma. The museum houses a classy collection of Oriental treasures, including the celebrated *Irises* screens, traditionally displayed for a month from the end of each April – expect big crowds for this popular exhibition. The museum's best feature, enjoyable any time of year and fully justifying the entrance fee, is its extensive garden, which slopes gently away around an ornamental pond. Dotted through it are several traditional teahouses, and mossy stone and bronze sculptures.

Meiji Memorial Picture Gallery

MAP P.80, POCKET MAP C7

聖徳記念絵画館, 1-1 Kasumigaokamachi. Daily 9am–5pm. ¥500.

At the northern end of a ginkgo-lined road is the **Meiji Memorial Picture Gallery**, featuring with a marble-clad entrance hall that soars up to a central dome. Inside are forty paintings depicting the life story of Emperor Meiji, of interest more for their scenes of Japan emerging from its feudal past than for their artistic merits.

Konnō Hachimangū

MAP P.80, POCKET MAP B9

金王八幡宮, 3-5-12 Shibuya. Shibuya station. Daily 24hr; buildings open 6am–5pm; ceremony daily 9am. Free.

One of the few bona fide sights in the Shibuya station area, the modest **Konnō Hachimangū** is of major importance. First established in 1092, though rebuilt many times since, the shrine was used as a place of worship by the Shibuya clan, who gave the area its present name. Their castle was once adjacent to the shrine, though only a couple of pieces of fortress stone are preserved on the site. Nevertheless, it's a pleasant escape from the noise of modern-day Shibuya; pop by for the morning ceremonies, if possible.

Cerulean Tower Noh Theater

MAP P.80, POCKET MAP B9

26-1 Sakuragaoka-chō. Shibuya station. ☎ 03 3477 6412, ⓦ www.ceruleantower-noh.com.

In the basement of the luxury *Cerulean Tower* hotel, this theatre provides an elegant setting for both professional and amateur nō and *kyōgen* performances (tickets typically ¥3500 and up).

Toguri Museum of Art

MAP P.80, POCKET MAP A9

戸栗美術館， 1-11-3 Shōto. Shibuya station. ☎ 03 3465 0070, Ⓦ www.toguri-museum.or.jp. Tues–Sun 10am–5pm; English-language tours 2pm. ¥1000 including tour; check website for discount admission coupons.

A little to the west of central Shibuya, the superb **Toguri Museum of Art** displays Edo-era and Chinese Ming-dynasty (1368–1644) ceramics. The small but exquisitely displayed exhibition, comprising selections from a collection of some 6000 pieces, is a must for those interested in pottery. Carefully positioned mirrors enable you to inspect the fine detail of work on the underside of displayed plates and bowls, and there's a pretty garden beside the lobby.

Japan Folk Crafts Museum

MAP P.80, POCKET MAP A9

日本民芸館， Tues–Sun 10am–5pm. Komaba-Tōdaimae station. ☎ 03 3467 4527, Ⓦ mingeikan.or.jp. ¥1100.

Two stops down the Keiō Inokashira line from Shibuya station is the outstanding **Japan Folk Crafts Museum**. Set in a handsome stone-and-stucco building five minutes' walk northwest of the station, the museum is a must-see for Japanese-craft fans, with an excellent collection of pottery, textiles and lacquerware. The gift shop is a fine source of souvenirs.

HARAJUKU AND SHIBUYA

The most loyal dog of all, Hachikō

Shops

Arts & Science

MAP P.80, POCKET MAP C9

6-6-20 Minami-Aoyama. Omotesandō
station. ☏ 03 3498 1091, 🌐 arts-science.
com. Daily noon–8pm.

Sonya Park, the Korean-born,
Hawaii-raised owner of this
boutique, has a great eye for
what works in fashion. Her
collection includes original pieces
alongside such things as sheepskin
Scandinavian army coats and
French perfumes.

Bapexclusive

MAP P.80, POCKET MAP C8

5-5-8 Minami-Aoyama. Omotesandō
station. ☏ 03 3407 2145, 🌐 bape.com.
Daily 11am–8pm.

A Bathing Ape, the streetwear
brand of designer Nigo, has a string
of boutiques all over Aoyama and
Harajuku, of which this is the main
showroom. One of their T-shirts
will set you back at least ¥6000.

Billionaire Boys Club

MAP P.80, POCKET MAP B8

4-5-21 Jingūmae. Meiji-jingūmae station.
☏ 03 5775 2633, 🌐 bbcicecream.com.
Daily 11am–7pm.

Boutique selling the hip-hop-
inspired clothes of Pharrell Williams
and the tutti-frutti-coloured sneaker
line Ice Cream (his collaboration
with Japanese designer Nigo, of A
Bathing Ape fame).

CA4LA

MAP P.80, POCKET MAP B8

1-18-2 Kaminami. Shibuya station. ☏ 03
3770 5051, 🌐 ca4la.com. Daily 11am–8pm.

Hat shop to the eternally trendy,
with everything from foppish
fedoras and broad-brimmed
sun hats to hip-hop beanies and
designer baseball caps. The name is
pronounced "Ka-shi-ra", by the way.

Chicago

MAP P.80, POCKET MAP B8

4-26-26 Jingūmae. Meiji-jingūmae station.

☏ 03 5414 5107, 🌐 www.chicago.co.jp.
Daily 11am–8pm.

There's a fine selection of kimono,
obi and so on at this Harajuku
thrift store, as well as rack upon
rack of good used clothes – plus
more at another branch, just along
the road.

Comme des Garçons

MAP P.80, POCKET MAP C8

5-2-1 Minami-Aoyama. Omotesandō
station. ☏ 03 3406 3951, 🌐 comme-des-
garcons.com. Daily 11am–8pm.

More like an art gallery than a
clothes shop, this beautiful store is a
suitable setting for the high-fashion
menswear and womenswear by
renowned designer Kawakubo Rei.

Gallery Kawano

MAP P.80, POCKET MAP C8

4-4-9 Jingūmae. Omotesandō station.
☏ 03 3470 3305. Daily 11am–6pm.

Excellent selection of vintage
kimono, yukata and obi, with
swatches of gorgeous kimono fabric
available too.

Hysterics

MAP P.80, POCKET MAP C8

5-5-3 Minami-Aoyama. Omotesandō
station. ☏ 03 6419 3899,
🌐 hystericglamour.jp. Daily noon–8pm.

The premier outlet for Hysteric
Glamour, a fun, retro-kitsch
Americana label which is one of
Japan's leading youth brands.

Issey Miyake

MAP P.80, POCKET MAP C8

3-18-11 Minami-Aoyama. Omotesandō
station. ☏ 03 3423 1407, 🌐 isseymiyake.
co.jp. Daily 11am–8pm.

One of the top names in world
fashion, famous for his elegant,
eminently wearable designs. This
flagship store, a pink building with
Art Deco touches, is suitably fancy.

Kiddyland

MAP P.80, POCKET MAP B8

6-1-9 Jingūmae. Meiji-jingūmae station.
T03 3409 3431, Wkiddyland.co.jp. Daily
10am–8pm, closed every third Tues.

Flagship store boasting six full floors of toys, stationery, sweets and other souvenirs.

Kura Chika Yoshida

MAP P.80, POCKET MAP B8
5-6-8 Jingūmae. Omotesandō station.
☎ 03 5464 1766, ⓦ www.yoshidakaban.com. Daily (except Wed) noon–8pm.
Access the full range of bags, wallets and luggage at this shrine to the hip Japanese brand Porter. It's just off Omotesandō, behind Tokyo Union Church.

Laforet

MAP P.80, POCKET MAP B8
1-11-6 Jingūmae. Meiji-jingūmae station.
☎ 03 3475 0411, ⓦ laforet.ne.jp. Daily 11am–8pm.
This pioneering "fashion building" is packed with boutiques catering to the fickle tastes of Harajuku's teenage shopping mavens. Wander through and catch the zeitgeist.

Mandarake

MAP P.80, POCKET MAP A9
31-2 Udagawachō. Shibuya station. ☎ 03 3477 0777, ⓦ mandarake.co.jp. Daily noon–8pm.
If you're into character dolls and plastic figures based on anime and manga, this subterranean operation is the place to head. They also have a wide range of secondhand manga as well as posters, cards and even costumes.

Musubi

MAP P.80, POCKET MAP B7
2-31-8 Jingūmae. Meiji-jingūmae station.
☎ 03 5414 5678. Daily (except Wed) 11am–7pm.
Pick up beautifully printed fabric *furoshiki* here to use instead of wrapping paper – they're also great gifts in themselves. Their origami design prints are particularly unusual.

Omotesando Hills

MAP P.80, POCKET MAP B8
4-12-10 Jingūmae. Omotesandō station.
☎ 03 3497 0310, ⓦ omotesandohills.com. Daily 11am–8pm.
Like a mini-mall for upscale local designers, this stylish, Andō Tadao-designed building is a must-visit for those with an interest in fashion.

Onitsuka Tiger

MAP P.80, POCKET MAP B8
4-24-14 Jingūmae. Meiji-jingūmae station.
☎ 03 3405 6671, ⓦ onitsukatiger.com. Daily 11am–8pm.
Selling trainers as seen on the most fashionable feet, this Japanese brand started business back in 1949. There are other branches across the city, including Ginza, Chou City and Shinjuku.

Prada

MAP P.80, POCKET MAP C8
5-2-6 Minami-Aoyama. Omotesandō station. ☎ 03 6418 0400, ⓦ prada.com. Mon–Thurs 11am–8pm, Fri–Sun 11am–9pm.
Without doubt the most attractive shop in Aoyama – which is saying something. Walk in like you own the place, head up to the top floor, and walk down the spiral stairs feeling like a superstar.

Laforet

Prada

Ragtag

MAP P.80, POCKET MAP B8
6-14-2 Jingūmae. Meiji-jingūmae station.
☎ 03 6419 3770, ⓦ ragtag.jp. Daily
11am–8pm.
A great place selling secondhand
goods from selected designers,
including local über-brands
Comme des Garçons, Yohji
Yamamoto and United Arrows.

Sou Sou

MAP P.80, POCKET MAP C9
5-4-24 Minami-Aoyama. Omotesandō
station. ☎ 03 3407 7877, ⓦ sousou.co.jp.
Daily 11am–8pm.
Cute range of modern design shoes
and clothes based on traditional
forms, such as split-toe *tabi* (socks).
Their plimsolls are an ideal match
for jeans.

Tōkyū Hands

MAP P.80, POCKET MAP A8
12-10 Udagawachō. Shibuya station.
☎ 03 5489 5111. Daily 10am–8pm, except
second and third Wed of the month.
This offshoot of the Tōkyū
department store is the place to
head if you're planning home
improvements or have practically
any hobby – they stock everything

you could possibly need, from
paper, paints and pencils to
backpacks and kayaks.

Tsumori Chisato

MAP P.80, POCKET MAP C8
4-21-25 Minami-Aoyama. Omotesandō
station. ☎ 03 3423 5170. Daily 11am–8pm.
Girlish streetwear that captures
the Harajuku look, but with better
tailoring, materials and attention
to detail.

United Arrows

MAP P.80, POCKET MAP B7
3-28-1 Jingūmae. Meiji-jingūmae station.
☎ 03 3479 8180, ⓦ united-arrows.co.jp.
Mon–Fri noon–8pm, Sat & Sun 11am–8pm.
Main store of the upmarket
fashion chain, famous for its
clean-cut men's shirts and suits.
Head to the top floor to have your
measurements taken for a custom-
made kimono or cotton shirt.

Village Vanguard

MAP P.80, POCKET MAP B9
23-3 Udagawa-chō. Shibuya station. ☎ 03
5281 5535. Daily 10am–11pm.
This "exciting bookstore" stocks an
amazing hotchpotch of toys and
novelties, from inflatable bananas to

Batman accessories – and a few fun books and CDs. You'll find quite a few branches around the city.

Yohji Yamamoto

MAP P.80, POCKET MAP C8
5-3-6 Minami-Aoyama. Omotesandō station. ☏ 03 3409 6006,
ⓦ yohjiyamamoto.co.jp. Daily 11am–8pm.
Flagship store of Japanese fashion icon Yohji Yamamoto, famed for his edgy, single-colour designs.

Cafés

Crisscross

MAP P.80, POCKET MAP C8
5-7-28 Minami-Aoyama. Omotesandō station. ☏ 03 6434 1266. Daily 8am–10pm.
One of Aoyama's "it" places, selling good coffee, and dessert dishes such as buttermilk pancakes (both from ¥900). For cheaper eats, pick up something from the adjoining Breadworks bakery.

Koffee Mameya

MAP P.80, POCKET MAP C8
4-15-3 Jingūmae. Omotesandō station.
☏ 03 5413 9422, ⓦ koffee-mameya.com.
Daily 10am–6am.
Something different in this café-infested area, and something like a laboratory for coffee. Prices are ¥550 and up, and the end results are wonderful, though sadly there's nowhere to sit.

La Fée Délice

MAP P.80, POCKET MAP B8
5-11-13 Jingūmae ☏ 03 5766 4084,
ⓦ lafeedelice.com. Mon–Sat 11.30am–11pm, Sun 11am–10pm.
The best of Harajuku's many crêperies – some chefs here have actually trained in France. Sweet and savoury crêpes go for ¥1080 and up.

Lion

MAP P.80, POCKET MAP A8
2-19-13 Dōgenzaka. Shibuya station. ☏ 03 3461 6858. Daily 11am–10.30pm.
Not the place for animated conversations, this *Addams Family*-style institution, set amid the love hotels of Dōgenzaka, is where businessmen bunking off work come to appreciate classical music with their coffee (¥550 and up). Seats are arranged to face a pair of enormous speakers.

L'Occitane

MAP P.80, POCKET MAP B9
2-3-1 Dōgenzaka. Shibuya station ☏ 03 5428 1564. Daily 10am–9pm.
This café above the eponymous cosmetics store has one huge draw – it's a prime viewing spot for Shibuya crossing. Thankfully, the coffee's fine; better, at least, than at the crammed Starbucks on the other side of the crossing.

Tokyo Snake Center

MAP P.80, POCKET MAP B8
8F Sanpo-Sogo Building, 6-5-6 Jingūmae.
Meiji-jingūmae station. ☏ 03 6427 9912,
ⓦ snakecenter.jp. Daily (except Tues)
11am–8pm.
One of the better "weird-animal" cafés in Tokyo, and decently priced at ¥1000 entry, including a drink; it's ¥540 more to pet a couple of small snakes.

Tearooms

The Alley Lujiaoxiang

MAP P.80, POCKET MAP B8
6-6-6 Jingūmae. Meiji-jingūmae station.
☏ 03 6712 5185, ⓦ the-alley.jp. Daily
10am–10pm.
Not so long ago it was buttermilk pancakes, but now if you see lengthy queues developing in Harajuku, it's most likely to be a bubble tea stand. For the actual tea, this one's best – just be prepared to wait a little while.

Aoyama Flower Market

MAP P.80, POCKET MAP C8
B1 5-1-2 Aoyama. Omotesandō station.
☏ 03 3400 0887, ⓦ afm-teahouse.com.
Daily 11am–8pm.
Yes, it's a flower shop – but one whose heady aromas also permeate

a fantastic tea-space, tucked away through a door at the back. They've a good range of herbal and green-tea concoctions on offer in the ¥750 range.

Restaurants

Florilège

MAP P.80, POCKET MAP C7

2-5-4 Jingūmae. Gaiemmae station. ☎ 03 6440 0878, ⓦ aoyama-florilege.jp. Daily (except Wed) 12pm–1.30pm & 6.30–8pm.
Chef Hiroyasu Kawate is something of a culinary superstar in Tokyo, and his fusion of Japanese and French tastes is something to behold, if you can afford it (¥6500 for a six-course lunch, ¥12,500 for an 11-course dinner).

Ganso Kujiraya

MAP P.80, POCKET MAP A9

2-9-22 Dōgenzaka. Shibuya station. ☎ 03 3461 9145, ⓦ www.kujiraya.co.jp. Mon–Fri 11am–2pm & 5–10.30pm, Sat & Sun 11.30am–11.30pm.
Like it or not, the Japanese have eaten whale meat for centuries, and this smart, surprisingly cheap venue is a good place to sample it; at lunch when you'll get a hearty set from ¥1000.

Harajuku Gyōzaro

MAP P.80, POCKET MAP B8

6-2-4 Jingūmae. Meiji-jingūmae station. ☎ 03 3406 4743. Mon–Sat 11.30am–4am, Sun 11.30am–11pm.
It's just over ¥300 for a round of succulent *gyōza* at this atmospheric dumpling spot; your choices are fried or boiled, and with or without garlic, and you can chase them down with draught beer.

Los Barbados

MAP P.80, POCKET MAP A8

41-26 Udagawachō. Shibuya station. ☎ 03 3496 7157. Daily (except Sun) noon–3pm & 6–11pm.
Under a large map of the Congo, the Africa-phile owner of this little *izakaya* whips up great food from across the African continent; lunch meals cost under ¥1000, and there are always vegan options.

Maisen

MAP P.80, POCKET MAP C8

4-8-5 Jingūmae. Omotesandō station. ☎ 03 3470 0071, ⓦ mai-sen.com. Daily 11am–10pm.
Located in an old bathhouse, this long-running *tonkatsu* restaurant serves up superb set meals from just ¥1580; prices dip under ¥1000 for lunch, though you'll probably have to queue for a while.

Murugi

MAP P.80, POCKET MAP A9

2-29-1 Dōgenzaka. Shibuya station. ☎ 03 3462 0241. Daily (except Fri) 11.30am–3pm.
In the heart of Shibuya's sleazeland, this curry restaurant has been serving distinctive Fuji-shaped rice mounds (¥1000) since 1951; the only problem is that they're only open for lunch.

Out

MAP P.80, POCKET MAP B9

2-7-14 Shibuya. Shibuya station. ⓦ out. restaurant. Tues–Sat 6pm–late, Sun 11am–2.30pm & 6pm–late.
A small and uncommonly focused restaurant, where there's only one dish on the menu (truffle pasta; ¥4000 with wine, ¥2900 without), and only Led Zeppelin on the sound system.

Ramen Nagi

MAP P.80, POCKET MAP B9

1-3-1 Higashi. Shibuya station. ☎ 03 3499 0390, ⓦ n-nagi.com. Mon–Sat 11am–11pm, Sun 11am–10pm.
There are a few interesting ramen selections available here (¥880 a bowl), including the "Midorio", made with basil and cheese. More regular varieties are served in a rich broth, topped with delicious pork slices and a heap of chopped spring onions.

Sakuratei

MAP P.80, POCKET MAP B7
3-20-1 Jingūmae. Meiji-jingūmae station.
☎ 03 3479 0039, ⓦ sakuratei.co.jp. Daily
11am–11pm.

Funky, cook-your-own *okonomiyaki*,
monjayaki and *yakisoba* joint.
Dishes start at ¥950, and feature
some quirky options such as
curry, Okinawan or pizza-style
ingredients. A good drinks selection
means it's a fun place at night.

Uobei

MAP P.80, POCKET MAP A9
2-29-1 Dōgenzaka ☎ 03 3462 0241;
Shibuya station. Daily 11am–midnight.

Intensely bright restaurant in
which your sushi is ordered by
touch screen, then delivered by rail
on automated plates – the only
humans you see are those who
point you to your table and take
your cash. Gimmicky, but a lot of
fun – not to mention cheap, since
sushi plates go from ¥108.

Bars and clubs

Blue Note

MAP P.80, POCKET MAP C9
6-3-16 Minami-Aoyama. Omotesandō
station. ☎ 03 5485 0088, ⓦ bluenote.co.jp.

Tokyo's premier jazz venue, part
of the international chain, attracts
world-class performers. Entry for
shows is ¥6000–10,000 (including
one drink) depending on the acts,
though prices hit the stratosphere
for the global stars. Events
most evenings.

Bonobo

MAP P.80, POCKET MAP C7
2-23-4 Jingūmae. Meiji-jingūmae or
Sendagaya stations. ☎ 03 6804 554,
ⓦ bonobo.jp.

Walk past this place in the daytime,
and you'll usually think it's nothing
more than a wooden house. Come
evening, however, it transforms
into a highly intimate club, with
a surprisingly good sound system.
Events most evenings.

Aoyama Flower Market

BYG

MAP P.80, POCKET MAP A9
2-19-14 Dōgenzaka. Shibuya station.
ⓦ www.byg.co.jp. Usually a few events
each week, 5.30pm–2am.

Tiny rock venue which has been
around since the late 1960s – the
acts often play music of a similar
vintage. Tickets ¥1500–5000.

Club Asia

MAP P.80, POCKET MAP A9
1-8 Maruyamachō. Shibuya station. ☎ 03
5458 2551, ⓦ clubasia.co.jp. Fri & Sat, and
sometimes Sun & Thurs.

A mainstay of the clubbing scene,
with the emphasis on techno
and trance nights, though they
occasionally wander into other
territories such as reggae and new
wave. A popular place for one-off
gigs by visiting DJs.

Club Quattro

MAP P.80, POCKET MAP A9
5F Quattro Building, 32-13 Udagawa-chō.
Shibuya station. ☎ 03 3477 8750, ⓦ club-
quattro.com.

Intimate rock music venue which
tends to showcase up-and-coming
bands and artists, though it also
plays host to well-known local and

international acts. Tickets ¥2000–4500. Events most evenings.

Coins Bar

MAP P.80, POCKET MAP A8

B1 Noa Shibuya Building, 36-2 Udagawa-chō. Shibuya station. ☎ 03 3463 3039. Daily 4pm–12.30am, later at weekends. This cool little basement bar offers most drinks for ¥320, making it a top choice if you're on a budget. Music is usually hip-hop and r'n'b; they also bring in DJs most weekends, when there's a ¥300 entry fee.

Commune 2nd

MAP P.80, POCKET MAP C8

3-13 Minami-Aoyama, Minato-ku. Omotesandō station. ⓦ commune2nd.com. Daily 11am–10pm; usually closed Dec–Feb. This outdoor court is a real hub of the area; most of the eateries sell drinks, including bottled local craft beer, but special mention should be made of Beer Brain, which doesn't

Club Quattro

do food at all (¥600 for a small draught beer).

Crocodile

MAP P.80, POCKET MAP B8

6-18-8 Jingūmae. Meiji-jingūmae or Shibuya stations. ☎ 03 3499 5205, ⓦ crocodile-live.jp. You'll find everything from samba to blues and reggae at this long-running basement space on Meiji-dōri, between Harajuku and Shibuya. Tickets ¥3000–4000. Events most evenings.

Far Yeast

MAP P.80, POCKET MAP B9

2-6-8 Shibuya. Shibuya station. ☎ 03 6874 0373, ⓦ faryeast.com. Mon–Fri 11.30am–3pm & 5–11pm, Sat & Sun 11.30am–10pm. Though it would be worth mentioning for the ace name alone, this is the best craft beer in the Shibuya area. There are usually up to a dozen beers on offer (¥1000 a glass), including their own blond, saison, pale and session ales.

Fight Club

MAP P.80, POCKET MAP A9

428 2-27-2 Dōgenzaka. Shibuya station. ☎ 03 3464 1799. Mon–Thurs 6pm–midnight, Fri & Sat 6pm–5am, Sun noon–6pm. Of Shibuya's array of weird bars, this is one of the oddest, featuring a functional kickboxing cage. You can spar there yourself for ¥1000, though staff will only allow you to do this before your drink (most priced at ¥500).

Gas Panic

MAP P.80, POCKET MAP B9

B1 21-7 Udagawachō. Shibuya station. ☎ 03 3462 9099, ⓦ gaspanic.co.jp. Daily 6pm–late. For many a year, the various *Gas Panic* clubs have, between them, constituted Tokyo's main meat markets, with this one the biggie. Free entry, cheap drinks, and lots of youngsters (both Japanese and foreign) doing things their parents wouldn't be proud of.

Goodbeer Faucets

MAP P.80, POCKET MAP A9

1-29-1 Shoto. Shibuya station. ☎ 03 3770 5544, ⓦ goodbeerfaucets.jp. Mon–Thurs 5pm–midnight, Fri 5pm–3am, Sat & Sun 1pm–midnight.

An excellent place for craft beer, selling over forty varieties on draught – some made by the Goodbeer brewery, others from across Japan and abroad. Large glasses cost ¥750–1300.

Harlem

MAP P.80, POCKET MAP A9

2-4 Maruyama-chō. Shibuya station. ☎ 03 3461 8806, ⓦ www.harlem.co.jp.

The city's prime hip-hop venue for two full decades, keeping abreast of the genre's undulations with a roster of young, energetic DJs. The crowd are almost all dressed to the nines – do likewise or you might as well not be here. Events most nights; sometimes closed Sun or Mon.

Karaoke-kan

MAP P.80, POCKET MAP A9

30-8 Udagawachō. Shibuya station. ☎ 03 3462 0785. Daily 24hr.

Japan's premier karaoke-box operator has branches liberally peppered across the capital. Rooms 601 and 602 in their Udagawachō branch were featured in the movie *Lost in Translation*. An hour of karaoke here costs from ¥900 per person, with a minimum order of one drink.

Legato

MAP P.80, POCKET MAP A9

15F E-Space Tower, 3-6 Maruyama-chō. Shibuya station. ☎ 03 5784 2121, ⓦ legato-tokyo.jp. Sun–Thurs 11.30am–2pm & 5.30pm–midnight, Fri & Sat 11.30am–2pm & 5.30pm–4am.

This fancy Italian restaurant's bar offers a memorable floor-to-ceiling view over Shibuya from fifteen floors up. Wines go from under ¥1000 a glass.

The Ruby Room

MAP P.80, POCKET MAP A9

2-25-17 Dōgenzaka. Shibuya station. ☎ 03 3780 3022, ⓦ rubyroomtokyo.com.

Cosy, unpretentious cocktail bar-club with frequent live music. Their open-mic night on Tuesdays (from 7pm) is a long-running affair that attracts a diverse crowd and throws up some talented performers. Events most nights.

Sound Museum Vision

MAP P.80, POCKET MAP A9

B1F 2-10-7 Dōgenzaka. Shibuya station. ☎ 03 5728 2824, ⓦ vision-tokyo.com.

1500-capacity club with four giant rooms, a bunch of regular club nights, and some seriously heavy sound systems. Their EDM events are best of all. Events Fri & Sat.

Tsutaya O-East

MAP P.80, POCKET MAP A9

2-14-8 Dōgenzaka. Shibuya station. ☎ 03 5458 4681, ⓦ shibuya-o.com.

This complex has several venues, all hosting live-music events, ranging from J-pop to hard rock. International bands also play here. Tickets from ¥2500. Events most nights.

Womb

MAP P.80, POCKET MAP A9

2-16 Maruyama-chō. Shibuya station. ☎ 03 5459 0039, ⓦ womb.co.jp.

Mega-club with a spacious dancefloor and pleasant chill-out space. Top DJs often work the decks, but be warned that at big events it can get ridiculously crowded. Events most nights.

WWW

MAP P.80, POCKET MAP A9

B1F Rise Building, 13-17 Udagawachō. Shibuya station. ☎ 03 5458 7685, ⓦ www-shibuya.jp.

Once an arthouse cinema, now featuing live music from a mixed bag of genres, from shoegaze to electronica, but they're all pretty high quality; all-night events sometimes take place in the upper level, and they sell out fast. Tickets from ¥2500. Events most nights.

Shinjuku and the west

No Tokyo neighbourhood has as evocative a name as Shinjuku, the very mention of which will conjure images of buzzing neon, teeming masses and drunken debauchery to anybody with more than a superficial knowledge of the city. Only 4km due west of the leafy tranquillity of the Imperial Palace, Shinjuku has a long and illustrious history of pandering to the more basic of human desires. This action-packed district has it all, from the love hotels and hostess bars of Kabukichō to shop-till-you-drop department stores and dazzlingly designed skyscrapers. Throw in robot performances, two-hour all-you-can-drink specials, Tokyo's main LGBTQ bar stretch and teeming covered arcades, and you've still only just scratched the surface.

Tokyo Metropolitan Government Building

MAP P.94, POCKET MAP A5

東京都庁, 2-8-1 Nishi-shinjuku; both observation rooms 45F. Tochōmae station. South observation room daily 9.30am–5.30pm; north observation room daily 9am–11pm; each observation room is closed a couple of days per month; free tours Mon–Fri 10am–3pm. Free.

Some 13,000 city bureaucrats clock in each day at the Gotham City-like **Tokyo Metropolitan Government Building** (TMGB), made up of twin 48-storey towers, an adjacent tower block, the Metropolitan Assembly Hall (where the city's councillors meet) and a sweeping, statue-lined and colonnaded plaza. The dense crisscross pattern of its glass and granite facade are reminiscent of both traditional architecture and the circuitry of an enormous computer chip. Both towers have **observation rooms**; it's worth timing your visit for dusk, so you can see Shinjuku's multicoloured lights spark into action.

NTT Intercommunication Centre NTT

MAP P.94, POCKET MAP A6

インターコミュニケーションセンター, 3-20-2 Nishi-Shinjuku. Hatsudai station. ☎ 03 5353 0900, ⓦ www.ntticc. or.jp. Tues–Sun 11am–6pm. Free, although usually ¥500 for special exhibitions.

The invariably fascinating **NTT Intercommunication Centre** is an innovative interactive exhibition space that seeks to encourage a dialogue between technology and the arts: past displays of high-tech art have included a soundproof room where you listen to your own heartbeat, and light-sensitive robots you can control with your brain waves. The free regular exhibitions change annually; the special exhibitions usually rotate monthly. On your way up, check out the Antony Gormley-designed statue, standing alone on the second floor.

Seiji Tōgō Memorial Sompo Japan Museum of Art

MAP P.94, POCKET MAP A5

損保ジャパン東郷青児美術館, 42F Sompo Japan Building, 1-26-1 Nishi-Shinjuku. Shinjuku, Nishi-Shinjuku or Shinjuku-nishiguchi stations. ⓦ sjnk-museum.org. Tues–Sun 10am–6pm. Fee varies by exhibition.

On the 42nd floor of the Sompo Japan Building you'll find the

Seiji Tōgō Memorial Sompo Japan Museum of Art, home to one in the series of *Sunflowers* paintings by Vincent van Gogh, flanked by other top-drawer Impressionist pieces by Cézanne and Gauguin. The *Sunflowers* canvas, dating from 1888, was bought for the then-astronomical sum of ¥5 billion (a shade under $40m) during the height of Japan's "bubble economy" years. More interesting and unusual is the collection of over two hundred pieces by Tōgō Seiji, a popular Japanese artist best known for his soft, contoured depictions of women.

PUK Theatre

MAP P.94, POCKET MAP A6

2-12-3 Yoyogi. Shinjuku station. ☎ 03 3370 5128, ⊕ puppettheatrepuk.wordpress.com.

This charming puppet theatre was founded in 1929 as La Pupa Klubo, and survived a government witch-hunt during the war. It's home to a resident group of puppeteers, as well as visiting troupes, and puts on shows that both young and old can enjoy.

Omoide Yokochō

MAP P.94, POCKET MAP A5

思い出横丁

Squashed up against the train tracks running north from the Odakyū department store is **Omoide Yokochō**, commonly known as Memories Alley. Lit by hundreds of *akachochin* (red lanterns), it's also known as Shomben Yokochō ("Piss Alley"), a reference to the time when patrons of the area's many cramped *yakitori* joints and bars relieved themselves in the street, for want of other facilities. Don't be put off: the alley remains a cheap and atmospheric place to eat and drink (and there are toilets these days).

Tokyo Metropolitan Government Building

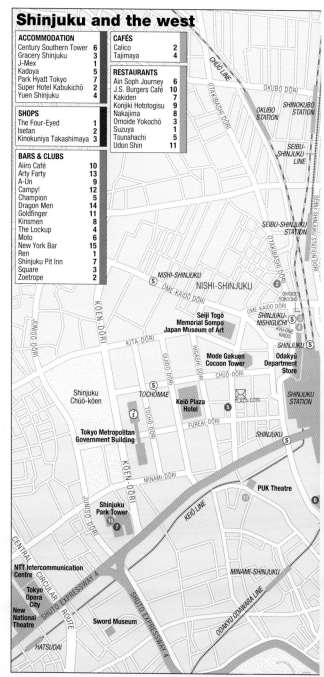

Shinjuku and the west

ACCOMMODATION
Century Southern Tower	6
Gracery Shinjuku	3
J-Mex	1
Kadoya	5
Park Hyatt Tokyo	7
Super Hotel Kabukichō	2
Yuen Shinjuku	4

SHOPS
The Four-Eyed	1
Isetan	2
Kinokuniya Takashimaya	3

BARS & CLUBS
Aiiro Café	10
Arty Farty	13
A-Un	9
Campy!	12
Champion	5
Dragon Men	14
Goldfinger	11
Kinsmen	8
The Lockup	4
Moto	6
New York Bar	15
Ren	1
Shinjuku Pit Inn	7
Square	3
Zoetrope	2

CAFÉS
Calico	2
Tajimaya	4

RESTAURANTS
Ain Soph Journey	6
J.S. Burgers Café	10
Kakiden	7
Konjiki Hototogisu	9
Nakajima	8
Omoide Yokochō	3
Suzuya	1
Tsunahachi	5
Udon Shin	11

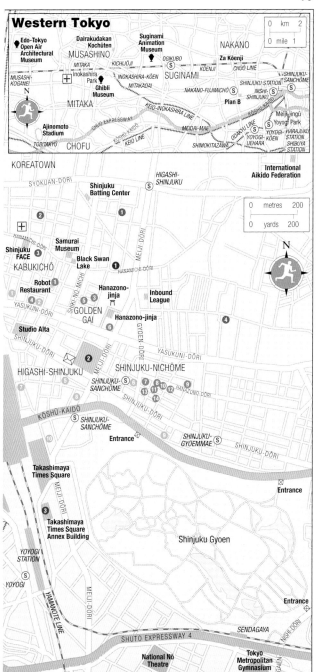

Kabukichō

MAP P.94, POCKET MAP B4–B5
歌舞伎町

The lively red-light district of
Kabukichō was named after a
never-built kabuki theatre that
was planned for the area in the
aftermath of World War II.
Although there have been plans
for redevelopment, the myriad
host and hostess bars, girly shows,
sex venues and love hotels are well
entrenched. For casual strollers
it's all pretty safe, thanks to street
security cameras. Take a wander
in the grid of streets around
Hanamichi-dōri and you can't
miss the peacock-preening young
Japanese male touts who hook
women into the male host bars,
and do notably less primped gents
who do likewise for hostess bars
– the *yakuza* who run the show
are there, too, though generally
keeping a much lower profile.

Samurai Museum

MAP P.94, POCKET MAP B5
サムライミュージアム, 2-25-6
Kabukichō. Shinjuku or Seibu-Shinjuku
stations. Ⓦ samuraimuseum.jp. Daily

10.30am–9pm. ¥1900, plus ¥500 to dress
up in samurai clothing.

In the modern **Samurai Museum**
you can check out displays of
samurai costumes and helmets,
and if you're willing to shell out
more on top of the already-hefty
ticket price you can don similar
togs yourself. If you time it right,
there are four daily "shows" in
which a genuine samurai actor
comes by to show off his sword-
wielding prowess.

Hanazono-jinja

MAP P.94, POCKET MAP B5
花園神社, 5-17-3 Shinjuku. Shinjuku,
Seibu-shinjuku, Shinjuku-sanchōme
stations. 24hr. Free.

Set in grounds studded with
vermillion *torii*, the attractive
Hanazono-jinja predates the
founding of Edo by the Tokugawa,
but the current granite buildings
are modern re-creations – the
shrine was originally sited where
the department store Isetan now
is. At night spotlights give the
shrine a special ambience and
every Sunday there's a flea market
in its grounds.

Samurai costumes on display inside the Samurai Museum

Shinjuku Gyoen

Golden Gai

MAP P.94, POCKET MAP B5
ゴールデン街
Just west of the Hanazono-jinja is **Golden Gai**, one of Tokyo's most atmospheric bar quarters. Since just after World War II, intellectuals and artists have rubbed shoulders with Kabukichō's demimonde in the tiny bars here; in recent years the area has undergone a mini-renaissance, with a younger generation of bar masters and mistresses taking over – or at least presiding over – some of the shoebox establishments. Many bars continue to welcome regulars only (and charge exorbitant prices to newcomers), but *gaijin* visitors no longer risk being fleeced rotten, since most places now post their table and drink charges outside the door.

Shinjuku Gyoen

MAP P.94, POCKET MAP B6–C6
新宿御苑, 11 Naitomachi. Main entrance Shinjuku-gyoenmae station; west gate Sendagaya station. Garden Tues–Sun 9am–4.30pm, last entry 4pm; villa second & fourth Sat of month 10am–3pm. ¥500. Rakū-tei Tues–Sun 10am–4pm. Tea ¥700.
The largest garden in Tokyo, and arguably the most beautiful, is **Shinjuku Gyoen**. Its grounds, which once held the mansion of Lord Naitō, the *daimyō* of Tsuruga on the Sea of Japan coast, became the property of the Imperial Household in 1868, and the garden was opened to the public after World War II.

Apart from spaciousness, the garden's most notable feature is the variety of design. The southern half is traditionally Japanese, with winding paths, stone lanterns, artificial hills and islands in ponds linked by zigzag bridges, and is home to *Rakū-tei*, a pleasant **teahouse**. At the northern end are formal, French-style gardens, with neat rows of tall birch trees and hedge-lined flowerbeds. Clipped, broad lawns dominate the middle of the grounds, modelled on English landscape design. On the eastern flank, next to the large

Dining with robots

Opened in 2012, the **Robot Restaurant** (ロボットレスト
ラン; 1-7-1 Kabukichō, Shinjuku station, ☎03 3200 5500,
🔗shinjuku-robot.com) is perhaps Tokyo's zaniest attraction,
and provides a little trip back to the wild days before Japan's
financial bubble burst. It all starts at the entrance foyer, where
there's nary an inch of regular, boring space – everything
glistens, shines, flashes or reflects. There's far more of the
same heading down the stairs to the trippy, video-screen-
lined hall where you'll be sat with other excited tourists and
locals. Though the website, and plenty of YouTube clips, will
give you a great idea of what to expect, the performances are
far more fun if you have no idea what's coming – for now, it
should suffice to say that dozens of robots, scantily dressed
girls, more LEDs than anyone could ever count, and a wall of
roaring music are on the cards. ¥8000 per head, plus ¥1000
(optional) for a light bentō meal. Performances run daily at
noon, 2pm, 4pm, 6.30pm & 8.30pm.

greenhouse, there's a replica of an
imperial wooden **villa** from 1869.
In spring, the garden bursts with
pink and white cherry blossoms,
while in early November
kaleidoscopic chrysanthemum
displays and golden autumn leaves
are the main attractions.

Suginami Animation Museum

MAP P.94, POCKET MAP A4
杉並アニメーションミュージア
ム, 3-29-5 Kamiogi. 🔗 sam.or.jp. Daily
(except Mon) 10am–6pm. Free. 20min walk
or 5min bus ride (platform 0 or 1; ¥220)
from Ogikubo station on the JR lines or
Marunouchi subway line.

Astroboy, Gundam and many
other anime characters are all
present and correct at the well-
organized **Suginami Animation
Museum**, situated atop a retro-
looking function hall. Colourful
displays trace the development
of animation in Japan, from the
simple black-and-white 1917
feature *Genkanban-no-maki* (The
Gatekeepers) to digital escapades
such as *Blood: The Last Vampire*.
Videos with English subtitles
explain how anime are made,
while interactive computer games

allow you to create your own
animations. You can watch anime
screenings in the small theatre,
and there's also a library packed
with manga and DVDs (some with
English subtitles).

Ghibli Museum

MAP P.94, POCKET MAP A4
ジブリ美術館, 1-1-83 Shimorenjaku.
☎0570 055777, 🔗 ghibli-museum.jp. Daily
(except Tues) 10am–6pm. ¥1000; advance
bookings only; 2400 tickets are available
per day (see website for details). Short
walk (follow signs) or bus ride (¥210) from
south exit of Mitaka station, on JR Chūō
line; or walkable from Kichijōji station,
also on JR Chūō line.

A few stops west of the Suginami
Animation Museum is the utterly
beguiling **Ghibli Museum**, one of
Tokyo's top draws for international
visitors – and an essential one for
those interested in anime. It's very
popular, so reserve tickets well
ahead of time. Though it needs
little introduction, the Ghibli
animation studio was responsible
for blockbuster movies including
My Neighbour Totoro, *Princess
Mononoke* and the Oscar-winning
Spirited Away. Visiting the
museum is a little like climbing

inside the mind of famed Ghibli director Hayao Miyazaki: walls are plastered with initial sketches of the characters that would eventually garner worldwide fame; a giant clock is bisected by a winding staircase; and – of course – there's the grinning cat-bus from *Totoro*. There's also a small movie theatre where original short animated features, exclusive to the museum, are screened. All in all, it's a guaranteed fun day out for all, that will probably have you scurrying to watch the films later.

Edo-Tokyo Open Air Architectural Museum

MAP P.94, POCKET MAP A4

江戸東京たてもの園, 3-7-8 Sakura-chō. ⓦ tatemonoen.jp. Daily (except Mon): April–Sept 9.30am–5.30pm; Oct–March 9.30am–4.30pm. ¥400. 5min bus ride (¥200) from Musashi-Koganei station, on JR Chūō line.

A kind of retirement home for old Japanese buildings, the **Edo-Tokyo Open Air Architectural Museum** was the inspiration for the abandoned theme park in Studio Ghibli's *Spirited Away*. Some 35 buildings of varying degrees of interest are gathered within the parkland of Koganei-kōen, plus an exhibition hall with archeological artefacts and folk crafts.

On the west side of the sprawling complex, check out the grand **Mitsue Residence**, an 1852 mansion moved from Kyoto and furnished with painted screens, lacquered shrines and chandeliers. There are also several thatched farmhouses. On the east side, there's a reconstructed **Shitamachi** street (see page 53), including a tailor's shop and stationer's, plus kitchenware and flower stores. The **public bathhouse** here is a veritable palace of ablutions, with magnificent Chinese-style gables and a lakeside view of Fuji painted on the tiled wall inside. Also look out for the **Uemura-tei**, a 1927 shophouse, its copper cladding pocked by shrapnel from World War II bombings.

Suginami Animation Museum

Shops

The Four-Eyed

MAP P.94, POCKET MAP B5

2-8-2 Kabukichō. Higashi-Shinjuku station. Ⓦ thefoureyed.shop. Daily 1–9pm.
This shop has an impeccably selected range of pricey menswear, but that's only half the story – it's set in a former love motel, off a hidden courtyard that can only be accessed by bypassing the lobby of another love motel (the *Avyss*): Kabukichō in a nutshell.

Isetan

MAP P.94, POCKET MAP B5

3-14-1 Shinjuku. Shinjuku-sanchōme station. Ⓣ 03 3352 1111, Ⓦ isetan.co.jp. Daily 10am–8pm.
One of the city's best department stores, with an emphasis on well-designed local goods and a reputation for promoting up-and-coming fashion designers. Their annexe, housing men's clothing and accessories, is particularly chic.

Kinokuniya Takashimaya

MAP P.94, POCKET MAP B6

Times Square, Annex Building, 5-24-2 Sendagaya, Shinjuku-ku. Shinjuku station. Ⓣ 03 5361 3301. Daily 10am–8pm; closed one Wed each month.
The sixth floor of Kinokuniya's seven-storey Shinjuku outlet offers Tokyo's widest selection of foreign-language books and magazines, including loads of Rough Guides.

Cafés

Calico

MAP P.94, POCKET MAP B5

6F, 1-16-2 Kabukichō. Shinjuku station. Ⓣ 03 6457 6387, Ⓦ catcafe.jp. Daily 11am–10pm.
A great place to experience the cat café phenomenon; ¥600 gets you thirty minutes of quality time with some fifty gorgeous kitties. With instructions and menu in English, it's very foreigner friendly, and offers inexpensive drinks and food. No kids under 12 are allowed.

Tajimaya

MAP P.94, POCKET MAP B5

Omoide Yokochō. Shinjuku station. Ⓣ 03 3342 0881. Daily 10am–10.30pm.
Surprisingly genteel for this ragged area of dining and drinking alleys, this elegant café serves quality drinks and cakes on a pretty assortment of china. Most coffees ¥720.

Restaurants

Ain Soph Journey

MAP P.94, POCKET MAP B5

3-8-9 Shinjuku. Shinjuku-sanchōme station. Ⓣ 03 5925 8908. Daily 11.30am–5pm & 6–10pm.
Popular, presentable vegan restaurant doling out salads, veggie soups, green curry and the like, all costing ¥1200 or so for lunch, and a bit more at dinnertime. They also make delectable vegan pancakes (¥1620).

J.S. Burgers Café

MAP P.94, POCKET MAP B5

3F 4-1-7 Shinjuku. Shinjuku station. Ⓣ 03 5367 0185, Ⓦ burgers.journal-standard.jp. Mon–Fri 11.30am–10pm, Sat 10.30am–10.30pm, Sun 10.30am–9pm.
A fab range of home-made chunky burgers, hot dogs and sandwiches are served at this retro-styled café – it's ¥1210 for a bacon-and-egg burger, and ¥1620 for the three-patty monster.

Kakiden

MAP P.94, POCKET MAP B5

8F Yasuyo Building, 3-37-11 Shinjuku. Shinjuku station. Ⓣ 03 3352 5121, Ⓦ kakiden.com. Daily 11am–9pm.
One of the best places in Tokyo to sample *kaiseki-ryōri*. There's a lunch set for ¥4320, but you won't regret investing in the eighteen-course dinner for ¥8640. They also conduct *kaiseki* appreciation classes.

Konjiki Hototogisu

MAP P.94, POCKET MAP B5
2-4-1 Shinjuku. Shinjuku-gyoemmae
station. ℡ 03 3373 4508. Mon–Fri
11am–3pm & 6.30–10pm.
There's always a long queue outside
this esteemed noodle restaurant.
Two types of ramen soba are
available, as well as a *tsukesoba*
(dry noodles with dipping stock),
and all cost under ¥1000, unless
you go for some of the highly
tempting add-ons.

Nakajima

MAP P.94, POCKET MAP B5
3-32-5 Shinjuku. Shinjuku station. ℡ 03
3356 4534, ⓦ shinjyuku-nakajima.com.
Daily (except Sun, 11.30am–1.45pm &
5.30–8.30pm).
At lunch all the delicious dishes
served here are made with sardines.
For dinner it's worth the expense
(over ¥8000 per person) to sample
the chef's Kansai *kapo* style of
cooking, similar to *kaiseki-ryōri*.

Omoide Yokochō

MAP P.94, POCKET MAP A5
1-2-7 Nishi-Shinjuku. Shinjuku station.
Most places daily 4pm–midnight.
It's almost pointless recommending
specific establishments on this
hugely atmospheric *yokochō* alley –
just stroll along a few times, until
you've spied both the food you
desire, and a free seat.

Suzuya

MAP P.94, POCKET MAP B5
Kabukichō Ichibangai-iriguchi.
Shinjuku station. ℡ 03 3209 4408. Daily
11am–10.30pm.
Famous *tonkatsu* restaurant, which
first opened just after World War
II. Their twist on the breaded pork
cutlet dish is to serve it *ochazuke*
style (¥1530) – you pour green tea
over the meat and rice to make a
kind of savoury porridge.

Tsunahachi

MAP P.94, POCKET MAP B5
3-31-8 Shinjuku. Shinjuku station. ℡ 03
3352 1012, ⓦ tunahachi.co.jp. Daily

Omoide Yokochō

11am–10pm.
This famous tempura restaurant
almost always has a queue outside.
Everything is freshly made, and
the bowls, cups and plates are
all little works of art. Even the
smallest lunch set (just over ¥1500,
including soup, rice and pickles)
will fill you up.

Udon Shin

MAP P.94, POCKET MAP A6
2-20-16 Yoyogi. Shinjuku station. ℡ 03
6276 7816. Sun–Thurs 11am–11pm, Fri &
Sat 11am–midnight.
Venerable udon joint where
most bowls cost ¥900–1300);
some options include flying-fish
tempura, others have a yuzu sauce,
and there's even a carbonara-like
choice with parmesan cheese and
bacon tempura.

Bars and clubs

AiiRO Café

MAP P.94, POCKET MAP B5
2-18-1 Shinjuku. Shinjuku-sanchōme

station. ☏ 03 3358 3988, Ⓦ aliving.net.
Daily 6pm–4am (Sun until 1am).
Many a night in Nichōme starts
with a drink at this LGBTQ bar,
and quite a few finish here too. The
bar itself is tiny, which is why scores
of patrons hang out on the street
corner outside, creating a block
party atmosphere on weekends.

Arty Farty

MAP P.94, POCKET MAP B5
2F Dai 33 Kyutei Building, 2-11-7 Shinjuku.
Shinjuku-sanchōme station. ☏ 03 5362
9720, Ⓦ arty-farty.net. Daily 6pm–1am.
As the night draws on, this
pumping LGBTQ bar's small
dancefloor gets packed with an
up-for-fun crowd. Their annexe
bar, within staggering distance, hits
its stride later in the evening and
draws a younger clientele.

A-Un

MAP P.94, POCKET MAP B5
3F 2-14-16 Shinjuku. Shinjuku-sanchōme
station. ☏ 070 6612 9014. Daily 6pm–2am,
Fri & Sat until 4am.
A quirky bar in many ways: it's
lesbian-friendly but doesn't mind

New York Bar

fellas coming in; the sound system
is unusually good; and you can
bring your own booze for ¥500.
Entry is usually ¥1000 including a
free drink.

Campy!

MAP P.94, POCKET MAP B5
2-13-10 Shinjuku. Shinjuku-sanchōme
station. ☏ 03 6273 2154. Daily 6pm–2am
(Fri & Sat until 4am).
This highly colourful venue is
perhaps the tiniest of the area's
many minuscule LGBTQ bars, but
what it lacks in size it makes up for
in pizzazz – the drag queen staff
sure help. One of the better local
venues for straight folk.

Champion

MAP P.94, POCKET MAP B5
Golden Gai, off Shiki-no-michi. Shinjuku-
sanchōme station. Mon–Sat 6pm–6am.
At the western entrance to the
Golden Gai stretch, this is the
largest bar in the area. There's no
cover charge and most drinks are a
bargain ¥500 – some even less. The
catch? You have to endure tone-
deaf patrons crooning karaoke for
¥100 a song.

Dragon Men

MAP P.94, POCKET MAP B5
2-11-4 Shinjuku. Shinjuku-sanchōme
station. ☏ 03 3341 0606. Daily 6pm–3am
(Fri & Sat until 5am).
The average Nichōme bar is
pretty tiny, but this is a relative
whopper – big enough for a proper
dancefloor. Good music, a street-
side terrace, daily happy-hour
specials and strong drinks served
by tattooed *gaijin* waiters clad only
in underpants.

Goldfinger

MAP P.94, POCKET MAP B5
2-12-11 Shinjuku. Shinjuku-
sanchōme station. ☏ 03 6383 4649,
Ⓦ goldfingerparty.com. Daily 6pm–2am
(Fri & Sat until 4am).
This fun, female-only bar is famed
for the regular wild parties it runs
and though these are actually held

elsewhere, the bar itself is a fun drinking hole, styled something like an old motel and presided over by glamourpuss DJs.

Kinsmen

MAP P.94, POCKET MAP B5
2F 2-18-5 Shinjuku. Shinjuku-sanchōme station. ☎ 03 3354 4949. Tues–Sun 8pm–1am (Fri & Sat until 3am).
Long-running and unpretentious bar – you're as likely to be carousing with a mixed group of office workers here as with a drag queen. Check out their famous *ikebana* – traditional flower displays.

The Lockup

MAP P.94, POCKET MAP B5
6/7F 1-16-3 Kabukichō. Shinjuku station. ☎ 050 5305 7370. Mon–Fri 5pm–midnight, Sat & Sun noon–midnight.
It's quite a trip merely walking into this house-of-horrors/prison themed bar – you'll be handcuffed then led to a cell-like room where you can take your pick of weird cocktails: some arrive in test tubes; others have fake eyeballs inside.

Moto

MAP P.94, POCKET MAP B5
5-17-11 Shinjuku. Shinjuku-sanchōme station. Mon–Fri 3–11pm, Sat noon–11pm.
One for the sake aficionados – there are usually 50–60 varieties for the tasting in this standing-only basement lair, and they're all excellent. Most cost just ¥380 per glass, making a tasting session almost inevitable.

New York Bar

MAP P.94, POCKET MAP A6
Park Hyatt Hotel, 3-7-1-2 Nishi-Shinjuku. Tochōmae station. ☎ 03 5322 1234, ⓦ tokyo.park.hyatt.jp. Evening shows start 8pm (7pm Sun).
Top-class live jazz, plus the glittering Shinjuku night views seen in *Lost in Translation*, are the attractions of this sophisticated bar atop the *Park Hyatt* (see page

116); the cover charge (¥2700) is waived if you eat there. Smart attire recommended.

Ren

MAP P.94, POCKET MAP B5
1-7-1 Kabukichō. Shinjuku-sanchōme station. ☎ 03 6273 9736. Daily 10pm–5am.
Shows at the *Robot Restaurant* are fantastic fun but rather overpriced. However, you can sample the surreal, wacky-and-tacky atmosphere at its sister bar, which opens up to non-customers after showtime. Drinks are surprisingly reasonable, going from ¥500.

Shinjuku Pit Inn

MAP P.94, POCKET MAP B5
B1F Accord Shinjuku Building, 2-12-4 Shinjuku. Shinjuku station. ☎ 03 3354 2024, ⓦ pit-inn.com.
Serious, long-standing jazz club which has been the launch platform for many top Japanese performers. Tickets cost ¥3000 in the evening, and less for daytime shows. Shows 2.30pm & 7.30pm most days.

Square

MAP P.94, POCKET MAP B5
2F 3rd Street, Golden Gai. Shinjuku-sanchōme station. Mon–Sat 6pm–4am.
Cute, squashed little upper-floor bar in Golden Gai (see page 97) with cheery staff, cheery customers, decent drinks, and some dangerous-looking bras on the wall. Look out for the blue sign, which is, ironically, a circle. Cover charge ¥500.

Zoetrope

MAP P.94, POCKET MAP A5
7-10-14 Nishi-Shinjuku. Seibu-Shinjuku station. ☎ 03 3363 0162. Mon–Sat Sun 7pm–4am.
The most vaunted whisky bar in the Shinjuku area, with umpteen varieties of foreign and Japanese scotch and single malts. Look for the small red sign with an eye and "shot bar" next to the *katakana*.

Ikebukuro and the north

Little more than marshland until the dawn of the twentieth century, Ikebukuro is a real product of the train age; eight lines now connect the area with central Tokyo and the low-cost dormitory suburbs to the north and east, meaning that its primary function is as a sort of commuter gateway to the city. It's not as trendy or hip as Shinjuku or Shibuya, and the area is also something of a byword for Tokyo sleaze, with its glut of "soaplands" (a particularly peculiar breed of brothels). However, stick around long enough and you'll find some of the city's best noodles, classic gardens to stroll in, a handful of butler cafés (see page 108) and some truly fascinating pieces of architecture. All in all, Ikebukuro and its environs provide a good window in which to see Tokyo simply being Tokyo.

Myonichi-kan

MAP P.106, POCKET MAP B1
明日館, 2-31-3 Nishi-Ikebukuro. Ikebukuro station. ☎ 03 3971 7535, Ⓦ jiyu. jp. Tues–Sun 10am–4pm, closed during functions. ¥400, or ¥600 including coffee/ Japanese tea and sweets.

Fans of the American architect Frank Lloyd Wright should track down one of his lesser-known but still very distinctive buildings, the **Myonichi-kan**, or "House of Tomorrow". While working on the *Imperial Hotel* near the Imperial Palace, Wright and his assistant Endo Arata also designed this complex to house the Jiyū Gakuen school. The geometric windows and low-slung roofs are trademark Wright features, but the buildings are best appreciated from inside, where you get the full effect of the clean, bold lines, echoed in the hexagonal chairs, light fittings and other original furnishings.

Sunshine Aquarium

MAP P.106, POCKET MAP C1
サンシャイン水族館, ☎ 03 5950 0765, Ⓦ sunshinecity.jp/aquarium. Daily 9am–9pm. Adult/child ¥2200/1200.

The wonderful **Sunshine Aquarium** is by far the best in Tokyo, with its rather high ticket price justified by inventive attractions, best of which are the "Sunshine Aqua Ring", where you'll be able to see sea-lions torpedoing around above your head, and the magical "Jellyfish Tunnel".

Namco Namja Town

MAP P.106, POCKET MAP C1
ナムコナンジャタウン, ☎ 03 5950 0765, Ⓦ event.bandainamco-am.co.jp. Daily 10am–10pm. With "passport" adult/ child ¥3500/2800; without "passport" adult/child ¥500/300.

Part of the Sunshine City complex, **Namco Namja Town** is a noisy indoor amusement centre based around a couple of cat characters. It's notable for its various themed eating areas, including sections specializing in *gyōza* (Chinese-style fried and steamed dumplings), ice cream (flavours have, in the past, included squid and shark), and desserts from around Japan. The "passport" allows unlimited access to fourteen of the attractions, which include a mosquito-zapping gun game, a fishing challenge and a zombie-hunting video game.

Chinzan-sō

POCKET MAP D2

椿山荘, 2-10-8 Sekiguchi. Waseda station (Sakura Tram line). ⓦwww.chinzanso.com. Daily 9am–8pm. Free.

The area's prime sight is the **Chinzan-sō**, a beautiful, expansive nineteenth-century garden set around a small pond. Though sandwiched between a wedding hall complex and the *Hotel Chinzansō*, it's surprisingly easy to ignore those two ugly buildings, and concentrate on the greener delights of the garden. St Mary's Cathedral (see page 105) is just across the road from the north entrance; if you swing by the south entrance after lunch, you may get to see "Rick", a giant horned tortoise out for a walk.

St Mary's Cathedral

POCKET MAP D2

東京カテドラル聖マリア大聖堂, 3-16-15 Sekiguchi. Waseda station (Toden-Arakawa line) or Gokokuji station. ⓦtokyo.catholic.jp. Daily 9am–5pm.

St Mary's Cathedral has been the centre of Tokyo's Catholic community for well over a century, with congregations a mix of foreigners and Japanese. The original Gothic structure was built in 1899, but burned down in the World War II air raids; the present building, designed by Tange Kenzō, was completed in 1964. Steel-clad and shaped like a giant cross, it's rather iconic, almost enough to count as a Tokyo must-see. Be sure to take a peek at the dramatic interior; dominated by a massive pipe organ at one end and a retro-futurist cross at the other, it brings to mind scenes from Fritz Lang's *Metropolis*.

Rikugi-en

POCKET MAP F1

六義園, 6 Honkomagome. Daily 9am–5pm, tearoom noon–4.30pm. Gardens ¥300; teahouse ¥300 (for tea), or ¥600 with a sweet. Entrance on Hongō-dōri, 5min south of Komagome station.

Komagome's most appealing sight is **Rikugi-en**, Tokyo's best surviving example of a classical Edo-period stroll garden. In 1695 the fifth shogun granted one of his high-ranking feudal lords, Yanagisawa Yoshiyasu, a tract of farmland to the north of Edo. Yanagisawa was both a perfectionist and a literary scholar: he took seven years to design his celebrated garden – with its 88 allusions to famous scenes, real or imaginary, from ancient Japanese poetry – and then named it Rikugi-en, "garden of the six principles of poetry", in reference to the rules for composing *waka* (poems of 31 syllables). After Yanagisawa's death, Rikugi-en fell into disrepair until Iwasaki Yatarō, founder of Mitsubishi, bought the land in 1877 and restored it as part of his luxury villa. The family donated the garden to the Tokyo city authorities in 1938, since when it has been a public park.

Unsurprisingly, few of the 88 landscapes have survived – the guide map issued at the entrance identifies a mere

St. Mary's Cathedral

eighteen. Nevertheless, Rikugi-en still retains its beauty, and is large enough to be relatively undisturbed by surrounding buildings and traffic noise; most take the opportunity to sample *matcha* and traditional Japanese sweets in the teahouse overlooking the lake from the west.

Kyū Furukawa Gardens

POCKET MAP F1

旧古河庭園, **1-27-39 Nishigahara, Kita-ku. Daily 9am–5pm. ¥150, museum ¥800. Entrance 5min uphill from Komagome station.**

Designed by Ogawa Jihei, a famed gardener from Kyoto, the **Kyū Furukawa Gardens** combine delightful Japanese-style grounds with an Italian-style terrace of rose beds and artfully shaped azalea bushes. The gardens cascade down the hill from the **Otani Museum**, set in a mansion designed in 1914 by British architect Josiah Conder,

who was also responsible for the similar Kyū Iwasaki-tei house and gardens in Ueno (see page 49). It's possible to take tea and cake in the mansion and to go on a tour of the rooms. The best times to visit are in late April, when the azaleas bloom, and in mid-May, when the roses are out in full force.

Somei Onsen Sakura

POCKET MAP F1

染井温泉桜, **5-4-24 Komagome. Komagome station. Daily 10am–11pm. ¥1300.**

Most of Tokyo's bathhouses are either small, bare-bones establishments costing next to nothing, or over-the-top mega-complexes costing way too much and giving little in the way of a traditional feel. Hooray, then, for the **Somei Onsen Sakura**, which strikes a nice halfway-house vibe: pleasantly "regular" in feel, it's a great example of the Japanese

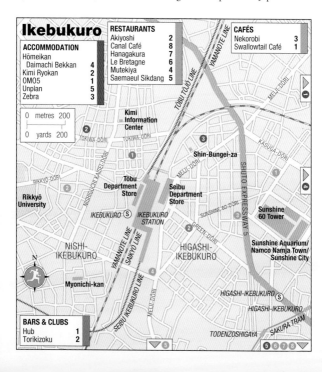

onsen experience. As you may have inferred from the name, it's best visited during cherry-blossom season, when the trees surrounding the site (though not actually visible from the baths) are cloaked with fluffy pink petals.

Tokyo Dome City Attractions

POCKET MAP G3

東京ドームシティ アトラクションズ, 1-3-61 Kōraku. Suidōbashi or Kōrakuen stations. ☎ 03 5800 9999, Ⓦ at-raku.com. Daily 10am–10pm. Individual rides ¥420–1030; "passport" with unlimited rides adult/age 12–17/age 6–11/age 3–5 ¥4200/3700/2800/2100, discounts after 5pm.

The best rides at the large **Tokyo Dome City Attractions** amusement park, part of the Tokyo Dome complex, are those in the LaQua section, where the highlight is Thunder Dolphin, a high-speed roller coaster guaranteed to get you screaming (for ages 8 and older). If you haven't got the stomach for that, try the Big O, the world's first hub-less and spoke-less Ferris wheel (it's spun by the two supports below), which provides a gentler ride and plenty of time to take a photo of the passing view. Tiny tots will enjoy Toys Kingdom, a space packed with playthings.

Spa LaQua

POCKET MAP G3

6F 1-1-1 Kasuga. Suidōbashi or Kōrakuen stations. Ⓦ www.laqua.jp. Daily 11am–9am (next day). Mon–Fri ¥2850, Sat & Sun ¥3170; ¥1940 surcharge 1am–6am; access to Healing Baden set of special therapeutic saunas ¥865 extra.

Spread over five floors, and part of the Dome City complex, **Spa LaQua** is by far the most sophisticated of Tokyo's bathing establishments (not to mention one of the most expensive), and is fed by onsen water pumped from 1700m underground.

Rollercoaster at Tokyo Dome City

Koishikawa-Kōrakuen

POCKET MAP F3

小石川後楽園, 1-6-6 Kōraku. Iidabashi station. ☎ 03 3811 3015, Ⓦ tokyo-park.or.jp. Daily 9am–5pm; English-language tours Sat 10am & 1pm. ¥300. Entrance in southwest corner of garden.

Immediately to the west of Tokyo Dome is **Koishikawa-Kōrakuen**, a fine, early seventeenth-century stroll garden. Winding paths take you past waterfalls, ponds and stone lanterns, down to the shores of a small lake draped with gnarled pines and over daintily humped bridges, where each view replicates a famous beauty spot. Zhu Shun Shui, a refugee scholar from Ming China, advised on the design, so Chinese as well as Japanese landscapes feature, the most obvious being the Full Moon Bridge, echoing the ancient stone bridges of western China, and Seiko Lake, modelled on the famed West Lake in Hangzhou. The garden attracts few visitors, though occasional squeals and rattles from the Tokyo Dome fairground rides, peeking up over the trees, mean it's not always totally peaceful.

Cafés

Nekorobi

MAP P.106, POCKET MAP B10
3F Tact TO Bldg, 1-28-1 Higashi-Ikebukuro.
Ikebukuro station. ☎ 03 6228 0646,
Ⓦ nekorobi.jp. Daily 11am–10pm.
This cat café has a minimum ¥1100
cover charge for the first hour
(¥1300 on weekends), which gets
you unlimited drinks, though most
go straight for the cat toys, and a
play with the felines.

Swallowtail Café

MAP P.106, POCKET MAP B10
B1F 3-12-12 Higashi-Ikebukuro.
Ikebukuro station. Ⓦ butlers-cafe.jp. Daily
10.30am–9pm.
A butler café where young
guys dressed like Jeeves are the
solicitous waiters in a room hung
with chandeliers and antique-
style furniture. Booking through
the (mostly Japanese) website is
essential. Expect to spend at least
¥2500 per head.

Nekorobi

Restaurants

Akiyoshi

MAP P.106, POCKET MAP A10
3-30-4 Nishi-Ikebukuro. Ikebukuro station.
☎ 03 3982 0601, Ⓦ akiyoshi.co.jp. Mon–Sat
5pm–midnight, Sun 5pm–11pm.
Unusually large *yakitori* bar with
a garrulous atmosphere and a
helpful picture menu. Most deep-
fried items are around ¥400 per
plate, and there's plenty of booze
on offer.

Canal Café

MAP P.106, POCKET MAP F4
1-9 Kagurazaka. Iidabashi station. ☎ 03
3260 8068, Ⓦ canalcafe.jp. Tues–Fri
11.30am–11pm, Sat & Sun 11.30am–9.30pm.
This is a surprisingly tranquil
and appealing waterside spot,
particularly romantic at night
when the old clapperboard
boathouses sparkle with fairy
lights. The café-restaurant has
decent-value pasta and pizza meals
(¥900–1400).

Yakitori served at Torikizoku

Hanagakura

MAP P.106, POCKET MAP E4

3-1 Kagurazaka. Iidabashi station. ☎ 03 3260 0767. Mon–Fri 11.30am–2.30pm & 5pm–midnight, Sat 11.30am–11pm.

There are tables everywhere you look in this rambling, atmospheric Kagurazaka restaurant. The food's wholesome Japanese fare, with the lunch deals especially good value (from ¥900).

Le Bretagne

MAP P.106, POCKET MAP E4

4-2 Kagurazaka. Iidabashi station. ☎ 03 3235 3500, ⓦ le-bretagne.com. Tues–Sat 11.30am–10.30pm, Sun 11.30am–10pm.

Attractive French-run restaurant offering authentic crepes (both sweet and savoury) from ¥780 and buckwheat *galettes* from ¥1180, as well as home-made Breton-style cider and good coffee.

Mutekiya

MAP P.106, POCKET MAP C1

1-7-1 Minami-Ikebukuro. Ikebukuro station. ☎ 03 3982 7656, ⓦ mutekiya.com. Daily 10.30am–4am.

The queue at this ramen joint often stretches a full 40m from the door – don't worry, since it moves along fairly quickly. While you wait you can decide on the size, flavour and toppings or your ramen or *tsukemen*; bowls start at ¥800 or so.

Saemaeul Sikdang

MAP P.106, POCKET MAP B4

1-1-4 Hyakuninchō. Shin-Ōkubo station. ☎ 03 6205 6226. Daily 11.30am–2am.

Tokyo outpost of an authentic Korean chain. Order some *yeoltan bulgogi* (like the meat from *shabu-shabu* without the soup, mixed with spicy paste; ¥950 per portion), and a boiling *doenjang jjigae* (a spicier, chunkier miso soup served with rice; ¥840 per portion).

Bars and clubs

Hub

MAP P.106, POCKET MAP B10

1-33-4 Nishi-Ikebukuro. Ikebukuro station. ☎ 03 3989 8682, ⓦ pub-hub.com. Mon–Thurs 5pm–1am, Fri 5pm–3am, Sat 4pm–3am, Sun 4pm–1am.

Always full enough to be fun, though with space to mingle, drinks are cheap at this bar, with cocktails going down to ¥190 during the 5–7pm happy hour; Western bar snacks are available too.

Torikizoku

MAP P.106, POCKET MAP C1

1-26-2 Minami-Ikebukuro. Ikebukuro station. ☎ 03 5944 9844. Daily 4pm–3.30am.

This chain has branches all over the city, but somehow the raucous vibe suits Ikebukuro best. Absolutely everything on the menu, whether food or drink, costs ¥298 (plus tax), or even less if you take advantage of their eat- and/or drink-all-you-can deals.

ACCOMMODATION

The Ōkura Tokyo

Accommodation

Tokyo's reputation for being an extremely expensive place to visit is justified as far as accommodation goes, but quality is generally very high at all levels, from luxury hotels to budget dorms. Staying at a traditional ryokan or a family-run minshuku can get you a highly local experience for a decent price; the same can be said for capsule hotels, which are certainly worth trying once. Staying in Tokyo will cost you from around ¥2500 for a hostel dorm bed (most prevalent around Asakusa), or ¥4000 for the very cheapest private rooms. You'll be looking at upwards of ¥10,000 for a more comfortable en-suite double in a business hotel. Mid-range hotels start in the region of ¥15,000, while top-end hotels charge at least twice that and often many times more. All hotel rates include 10 percent consumption tax, on top of which top-end hotels levy a service charge, typically 10 percent.

The Imperial Palace and around

HOSHINOYA MAP P.26, POCKET MAP H7. 1-9-1 Ōtemachi ☎ 050 3786 1144, ⓦ hoshinoyatokyo.com. A top-end hotel with ryokan-like elements to its decor and service; despite being seventeen floors high, it feels rather intimate, and the scent of flowers and incense wafts through the common areas. **¥80,000**

IMPERIAL HOTEL MAP P.26, POCKET MAP G7. 1-1-1 Uchisaiwai-chō ☎ 03 3504 1111, ⓦ imperialhotel.co.jp. Facing the Imperial Palace, this remains one of Tokyo's most prestigious addresses, with butler service on some floors, and no fewer than thirteen top-class restaurants. **¥50,000**

THE PENINSULA MAP P.26, POCKET MAP G7. 1-8-1 Yūrakuchō ☎ 03 6270 2288, ⓦ peninsula.com. Elegantly designed luxury hotel with an unbeatable location – offering views right across to the emperor's pad – and some of the city's most spacious rooms. **¥76,000**

TOKYO STATION MAP P.26, POCKET MAP H6. 1-9-1 Marunouchi ☎ 03 5220 1111, ⓦ www.thetokyostationhotel.jp. Grand old dame dating back to 1915, but given a mammoth, Euro-chic refurb along the lines of London's St Pancras' *Renaissance Hotel*. **¥47,000**

Ginza and around

CONRAD TOKYO MAP P.34, POCKET MAP G8. 1-9-1 Higashi-Shinbashi ☎ 03 6388 8000, ⓦ conradtokyo. co.jp. Luxury hotel with views that really steal the show – from the lobby and bayside rooms, feast your eyes on what are arguably the best vistas in Tokyo. They're especially magical in the evening. **¥64,000**

FOUR SEASONS MAP P.34, POCKET MAP H7. Pacific Century Place, 1-11-1 Marunouchi ☎ 03 5222 7222, ⓦ fourseasons.com/tokyo. They provide a pleasing personal touch at this luxuriant hotel – with a little warning, someone will be there on the platform to greet you at nearby Tokyo station. **¥82,000**

Booking ahead

Whatever your budget, it's wise to reserve your first few nights' accommodation before arrival. This is especially true of the cheaper places, which tend to fill up quickly, particularly over national holidays (see page 125), holiday periods, and cherry-blossom season (late March and early April). Good deals can be found online via hotel websites and general booking engines.

GINZA BAY HOTEL MAP P.34, POCKET MAP H8. 7-13-15 Ginza ℗ 03 6226 1078, ⓦ bay-hotel.jp. Capsule hotel designed with far more than usual, with little flourishes such as gorgeous pine fittings in the bathing areas, and USB ports in the pods. ¥3800

IMANO TOKYO GINZA MAP P.34, POCKET MAP H7. 1-5-10 Shintomi ℗ 03 5117 2131, ⓦ imano.jp. The Ginza area finally has a decent hostel, which somehow manages to look quite swanky. The second-floor lounge is a great hang-out spot. Dorms ¥3400, twins ¥10,000

MITSUI GARDEN GINZA MAP P.34, POCKET MAP H8. 8-13-1 Ginza ℗ 03 3543 1131, ⓦ www.gardenhotels.co.jp. Chic hotel boasting rooms decorated with great attention to detail, but it's the bird's-eye views of the city and bay that grab the attention – quite spectacular from each and every room. ¥27,500

MUJI HOTEL MAP P.34, POCKET MAP H7. 3-3-5 Ginza ℗ 03 3538 6101, ⓦ hotel.muji.com. The homeware behemoth made its first foray into the Japanese accommodation market in 2019, with its rooms sleek, accordingly minimalist and leaning on Japanese traditional design. ¥27,000

RYŪMEIKAN TOKYO MAP P.34, POCKET MAP H6. 1-3-22 Yaesu ℗ 03 3271 0971, ⓦ ryumeikan-tokyo.jp. This long-standing traditional inn has transformed into a stylish hotel, each room mixing Western comfort with attractive Japanese touches, accented in Edo-period purple (*edomurasaki*). ¥37,000

Akihabara and around

CITAN MAP P.42, POCKET MAP J5. 15-2 Nihambashiodenma-chō ℗ 03 6661 7559, ⓦ backpackersjapan.co.jp. The best hostel choice in the wider Akihabara area, a little slice of hipster paradise that's basically a two-star hotel. Dorms ¥3000, twins ¥9000

GLANSIT AKIHABARA MAP P.42, POCKET MAP H4. 4-4-6 Sotokanda ℗ 03 3526 3818, ⓦ glansit.jp. The lobby of this upscale capsule hotel would put many hotels to shame, and the snazzy design continues all the way to the berths and wonderful bathing facilities. ¥5000

HILLTOP MAP P.42, POCKET MAP G4. 1-1 Kanda-Surugadai ℗ 03 3293 2311, ⓦ yamanoue-hotel.co.jp. Perched on a small rise above Meiji University, this small 1930s hotel was formerly a haunt of famous writers. There are Art Deco touches and a friendly welcome. ¥24,000

JURAKU MAP P.42, POCKET MAP H4. 2-9 Kanda-Awajichō ℗ 03 3271 7222, ⓦ hotel-juraku.co.jp/ocha. Super little place coming across as something like a four-star, with a quirky, faux-industrial facade and a smart, honey-toned lobby. ¥17,000

Ueno and around

COCO GRAND UENO SHINOBAZU MAP P.48, POCKET MAP H3. 2-12-14 Ueno ℗ 03 3834 6221, ⓦ cocogrand.co.jp/uenoshinobazu. Reliable hotel with a choice of Western- or Japanese-style rooms, many with great views across Shinobazu pond. ¥19,000

GRAPHY NEZU MAP P.48, POCKET MAP H2. 4-5-10 Ikenohata ℗ 03 3828 7377, ⓦ hotel-graphy.com. Converted from a small apartment block, this is a great choice, with English-speaking staff, communal kitchen facilities, and well-appointed rooms. Locals often mingle with guests in the café-bar. ¥11,000

HANARE MAP P.48, POCKET MAP H1. 3-10-25 Yanaka ☏ 03 5834 7301, ⓦ hanare.hagiso.jp. Although marketing itself as a hotel, this is more like a ryokan in nature, with five old-school tatami rooms, tucked into the quirky Yanaka area. ¥10,500

NOHGA MAP P.48, POCKET MAP J3. 2-21-10 Higashi-Ueno ☏ 03 5816 0211, ⓦ nohgahotel.com. This boutique hotel stands out for its artistic leanings – many of the works you'll see around the hotel rotate in the manner of gallery exhibitions. Rooms are suitably attractive. ¥15,000

RYOKAN SAWANOYA MAP P.48, POCKET MAP H2. 2-3-11 Yanaka ☏ 03 3822 2251, ⓦ sawanoya.com. Welcoming, family-run inn in a convivial neighbourhood near Ueno Park. Though nothing fancy, the two lovely Japanese-style baths more than compensate. Singles ¥5600, doubles ¥10,600

Asakusa

1980 HOSTEL MAP P.54, POCKET MAP K1. 3-10-10 Shitaya ☏ 03 6240 6027, ⓦ 1980stay.com. The numbers in the name are the price you pay – this is basically the cheapest hostel in Tokyo, and its capsule-like beds are just fine. Dorms ¥1980

ASAKUSA CENTRAL MAP P.54, POCKET MAP B11. 1-5-3 Asakusa ☏ 03 3847 2222, ⓦ pelican.co.jp/asakusacentralhotel. Modest business hotel with a convenient location on Asakusa's main street, and small but well-appointed rooms. ¥14,000

BUNKA HOSTEL MAP P.54, POCKET MAP A11. 1-13-5 Asakusa ☏ 03 5806 3444, ⓦ bunkahostel.jp. Remarkably stylish hostel with comfy, curtained-off berths adding some rare privacy to the dorm experience. The lobby bar is a real winner, too. Dorms ¥3550

KHAOSAN TOKYO ORIGAMI MAP P.54, POCKET MAP B11. 3-4-12 Asakusa ☏ 03

3871 6678, ⓦ khaosan-tokyo.com. Part of the *Khaosan* hostel chain, with rooms given Japanese stylings, and a fair few paper cranes around the place. There are grand views of Asakusa from the lounge. Dorms ¥3800, doubles ¥10,000

NEW KOYO MAP P.54, POCKET MAP K1. 2-26-13 Nihonzutsumi ☏ 03 3873 0343, ⓦ newkoyo.com. Tiny little place with some of the cheapest private rooms in Tokyo; a bit out of the way, but within walking distance of Asakusa. Singles ¥2900, doubles ¥5200

RYOKAN SHIGETSU MAP P.54, POCKET MAP B11. 1-31-11 Asakusa ☏ 03 3843 2345, ⓦ shigetsu.com. This smart little ryokan is a haven of kimono-clad receptionists and tinkling *shamisen* music; there's a Japanese bath on the top floor, with views over temple roofs. Western singles ¥8000, tatami twins ¥17,000

SAKURA HOSTEL MAP P.54, POCKET MAP B11. 2-24-2 Asakusa ☏ 03 3847 8111, ⓦ sakura-hostel.co.jp. Friendly, well-run hostel a couple of minutes' walk northwest of Sensō-ji. Dorms ¥3300, twins ¥9300

SUKEROKU-NO-YADO SADACHIYO MAP P.54, POCKET MAP A11. 2-20-1 Asakusa ☏ 03 3842 6431, ⓦ sadachiyo. co.jp. Step back into Edo-era Asakusa in this delightful old inn. The elegant tatami rooms are all en suite, though you can also use the traditional Japanese-style baths. ¥21,600

Ryōgoku and Kiyosumi

ANNE HOSTEL MAP P.42, POCKET MAP K4. 2-21-14 Yanagibashi ☏ 03 5829 9090, ⓦ j-hostel.com. A lovely little place: part hostel, part traditional minshuku, with prices including a decent breakfast. It's a sociable place, but not party-crazy – a good option for solo travellers. Dorms ¥2600, twins ¥6800

NUI HOSTEL MAP P.42, POCKET MAP K4. 2-14-13 Kuramae ☏ 03 6240 9854, ⓦ backpackersjapan.co.jp/nui. This hostel's funky bar is a great mingling spot; the dorms aren't quite as fancy, but they do the job. Dorms ¥3000, doubles ¥7600

Bayside Tokyo

GRAND NIKKŌ MAP P.61, POCKET MAP A20. 2–6–1 Daiba ☎ 03 5500 6711, ⓦ tokyo.grand-nikko.com. Rising up over the bay, this luxurious hotel has walls peppered with contemporary art, and spacious rooms with great views of the Rainbow Bridge and the city beyond. ¥51,000

Akasaka and Roppongi

ANA INTERCONTINENTAL TOKYO MAP P.66, POCKET MAP E8. 1–12–33 Akasaka ☎ 03 3505 1111, ⓦ anaintercontinental-tokyo.jp. Offering great views across to Tokyo Midtown and the National Diet Building, this stylish hotel features a swimming pool and scores of restaurants. ¥42,000

THE B ROPPONGI MAP P.66, POCKET MAP E8 3–9–8 Roppongi ☎ 03 5412 0451, ⓦ roppongi.theb-hotels.com. A boutique-style hotel that won't break the bank or offend the eyes, even if uninspiring plastic-unit bathrooms are the norm throughout. ¥19,500

THE GLANZ MAP P.66, POCKET MAP E9. 2–21–3 Azabu-Jūban ☎ 03 3455 7770, ⓦ theglanz.jp. Highly appealing option with sleek, designer-style rooms including spa-style bathrooms and glimpses of Tokyo Tower. ¥15,000

GRAND HYATT TOKYO MAP P.66, POCKET MAP D9. 6–10–3 Roppongi ☎ 03 4333 1234, ⓦ tokyo.grand.hyatt. jp. Glamour is the order of the day at this big-player hotel. The rooms' appealing design uses wood and earthy-toned fabrics, and restaurants and bars are all very chic. ¥62,000

KAISU MAP P.66, POCKET MAP E8. 6–13–5 Akasaka ☎ 03 5797 7711, ⓦ kaisu.jp. One of the only hostels in the club-heavy Roppongi area – not a party hostel, but a beautiful place set into an old geisha house. They do, however, also have an excellent on-site bar. Dorms ¥4300

ŌKURA MAP P.66, POCKET MAP F8. 2–10–4 Toranomon ☎ 03 3582 0111, ⓦ www.hotelokura.co.jp/tokyo. Although only one wing remains of the iconic Ōkura, it remains a Tokyo classic with its 1970s time-warp lobby and beguiling garden view. The rooms are more contemporary. ¥49,000

THE RITZ-CARLTON MAP P.66, POCKET MAP E8. Tokyo Midtown, 9–7–1 Akasaka ☎ 03 6434 8100, ⓦ ritzcarlton.com. Occupying the top nine floors of the 53-floor Midtown Tower, this ultra-luxury hotel has a more contemporary look than usual for a Ritz-Carlton. ¥81,000

Ebisu, Meguro and the south

AKIMOTO MAP P.74, POCKET MAP B15. 3–2–8 Nakameguro ☎ 03 3711 4553. This minshuku is a super little find in fashionable Nakameguro, with small tatami rooms (not en-suite) and a general air of calm. Singles ¥2800, doubles ¥4000

DORMY INN MAP P.74, POCKET MAP A14. 3–21–8 Aobadai ☎ 03 3760 2211. By the banks of the delightful Meguro-gawa, rooms at this business hotel have a hotplate and small fridge; there's also a large communal bathroom and sauna, plus free bike rental. ¥17,000

RYOKAN SANSUISŌ MAP P.74, POCKET MAP D16. 2–9–5 Higashi-Gotanda ☎ 03 3441 7475, ⓦ sansuiso.net. Modest, beautifully maintained ryokan with simple tatami rooms, some with en-suite bath. Singles ¥5500, doubles ¥9200

THE STRINGS MAP P.74, POCKET MAP D16. 2–16–1 Konan ☎ 03 4562 1111, ⓦ intercontinental-strings.jp. Watch the Shinkansen come and go from this chic eyrie's airy atrium lobby; its combination of water, wood and stone evokes traditional Japanese design in a contemporary way. ¥35,000

ACCOMMODATION

Harajuku, Aoyama and Shibuya

CARAVAN TOKYO MAP P.80, POCKET MAP C8. 3–13 Minami-Aoyama ☎ 080 4145 3422, ⓦ caravantokyo.com. Glamping in Tokyo, made possible at this custom-built caravan; mod-cons include a/c, heating, a shower and a real bed. ¥15,000

CERULEAN TOWER TŌKYŪ HOTEL MAP P.80, POCKET MAP A9. 26–1 Shibuya-ku ☎ 03 3476 3000, ⓦ ceruleantower-hotel. com. Shibuya's ritziest rooms, some featuring bathrooms with glittering views of the city. Features a pool and gym, and even a jazz club and nō theatre. ¥52,000

GRANBELL MAP P.80, POCKET MAP B9. 15–17 Sakuragaoka-chō ☎ 03 5457 2681, ⓦ granbellhotel.jp. This boutique hotel has a hip feel, courtesy of curtains with Lichtenstein-style prints, kettles and TVs from a trendy local electronics range, and a neutral palette of crisp whites and natural colours. ¥22,000

THE MILLENNIALS SHIBUYA MAP P.80, POCKET MAP B8. 1–20–13 Jinnan ☎ 03 6824 9410, ⓦ themillennials.jp. One of the new breed of stylish capsule hotels, and a real hit with younger travellers. Most pods have been given artistic makeovers, and happy hour in the lobby gives guests a chance to mingle. ¥10,000

TRUNK MAP P.80, POCKET MAP B8. 5–31 Jingu-mae ☎ 03 5766 3210, ⓦ trunk-hotel.com. This boutique offering rises in stylish, sharp-edged layers from the side-road it calls home. Rooms are filled with art and local cosmetics, and the lounge often hosts parties on weekends. ¥35,000

TURNTABLE HOSTEL MAP P.80, POCKET MAP A9.10–3 Shinsen-chō ☎ 03 3461 7733, ⓦ turntable.tokyo. The best hostel option in the Shibuya area, a chic, hipster-friendly place whose dorms are slightly capsule-like in nature. There are socialising spots even within the corridors. Dorms ¥4500

Shinjuku and the west

CENTURY SOUTHERN TOWER MAP P.94, POCKET MAP B6. 2–2–1 Yoyogi ☎ 03 5354 0111, ⓦ southerntower.co.jp. Smart, stylish place that's better value than similar options in Nishi-Shinjuku. Come evening time, the views overlooking the station lend the place a *Blade Runner*-ish feel. ¥29,000

GRACERY SHINJUKU MAP P.94, POCKET MAP B5. 1–19–1 Kabukichō ☎ 03 6833 2489, ⓦ shinjuku.gracery.com. The famous "Godzilla hotel" that you may have spotted on your walk around Shinjuku; despite this, and the stylish rooms, it's surprisingly affordable. ¥21,000

J-MEX MAP P.94, POCKET MAP B4. 2–5–6 Kabukichō ☎ 03 3205 2223. This love hotel stands out from the crowd in Kabukichō; the racy rooms all have big TVs and karaoke machines, as well as built-in sauna units, and glowing spa tubs. "Rest" from ¥5800, "stay" from ¥11,500

KADOYA MAP P.94, POCKET MAP A5. 1–23–1 Nishi-Shinjuku ☎ 03 3346 2561, ⓦ kadoya-hotel.co.jp. Little charmer of a business hotel; rooms are a bargain given the location, and there's a lively *izakaya* in the basement. ¥16,000

PARK HYATT TOKYO MAP P.94, POCKET MAP A6. 3–7–1–2 Nishi-Shinjuku ☎ 03 5322 1234, ⓦ tokyo.park.hyatt. jp. Occupying the upper section of Tange Kenzō's Shinjuku Park Tower, this is the epitome of sophistication its huge rooms have breathtaking views, as do the restaurants, spa, pool and fitness centre. ¥74,000

SUPER HOTEL KABUKICHŌ MAP P.94, POCKET MAP B4. 2–39–9 Kabukichō ☎ 03 6855 9000, ⓦ superhoteljapan. co.jp. A budget treat, with rather beautiful communal bathing areas, and a surprisingly generous free breakfast. ¥12,000

YUEN SHINJUKU MAP P.94, POCKET MAP C5. 5–3–18 Shinjuku ☎ 03 5361 8355, ⓦ ryokan-yuen.jp. This "onsen ryokan" combines traditional styling with modern-day luxury, topped with onsen pools providing gorgeous views of Shinjuku. **¥15,500**

Ikebukuro and the north

HŌMEIKAN DAIMACHI BEKKAN MAP P.106, POCKET MAP G3. 5–12–9 Hongō ⓘ 03 3811 1187, ⓦ homeikan.com. Real looker of a ryokan, with ancient carpentry and traditional design. No en-suite bathrooms, but all rooms have tatami mats and look out on an exquisite little Japanese garden. **¥13,000**

KIMI RYOKAN MAP P.106, POCKET MAP A10. 2–36–8 Ikebukuro ⓘ 03 3971 3766, ⓦ kimi-ryokan.jp. A great-value institution on Tokyo's budget scene, and a good place to meet fellow travellers. There's a 1am curfew. Singles **¥5400**, doubles **¥8100**

OMO5 MAP P.106, POCKET MAP C10. 2–26–1 Kita-Ōtsuka ⓘ 03 5961 4131, ⓦ omo-hotels.com. New hotel appealing to youthful tastes, with a relaxed vibe, spacious duplex rooms and a snazzy common lounge. **¥13,000**

UNPLAN MAP P.106, POCKET MAP E3. 23–1 Tenjinchō ⓘ 03 6457 5171, ⓦ unplan. jp. One of the wave of flashpacker hostels offering capsule-like dorm "rooms"; set in pine frames and concealed by curtains, they're quite cosy. Dorms **¥4500**

ZEBRA MAP P.106, POCKET MAP B10. 1–37–1 Higashi-Ikebukuro ⓘ 03 3986 5015, ⓦ hotel-zebra.net. Set amidst the "soaplands" of Ikebukuro, this love hotel is adorned with all sorts of buttons, spikes and glowing panels. There are costumes to borrow in the lobby. "Rest" from **¥4800**, "stay" from **¥7800**

ESSENTIALS

Shimbashi street scene

Arrival

Tokyo boasts two major international airports: Narita, the old stalwart out east; and Haneda, far more central, recently upgraded, and hosting an ever-greater range of international connections. Other access points to the city include a slew of train stations and long-distance bus terminals, all for domestic connections only.

By air

Narita International Airport (ⓦwww. narita-airport.jp) is some 66km east of the city centre. The fastest way into Tokyo is on the **Skyliner** express train (1–3 hourly, 7.30am–10.30pm; 41min to Ueno; ¥2470; ⓦkeisei.co.jp); Keisei also offer the cheapest train connection into town (every 30min; 6am–11pm; 1hr 11min to Ueno; ¥1030). JR's **Narita Express** runs to several city stations, including Tokyo station, Shibuya, Shinjuku and Ikebukuro (7.45am–9.45pm; 1hr; ¥3020–3190; ⓦjreast.co.jp); for foreign passport holders, return tickets valid for two weeks cost ¥4000. Cheaper, but far less comfortable, JR trains run to Tokyo station (hourly; 1hr 25min; ¥1320).

The cheapest way into Tokyo is on the **Access Narita buses** (ⓦaccessnarita. jp; 7.30am–11pm), which head to Ginza and Tokyo stations, and cost just ¥1000; departing every 15min at peak times, they even have toilets on board, but they can be prone to traffic delays. You can pay with cash on the bus; check the website for boarding points. Taxis to central Tokyo cost over ¥20,000, and save little time.

Just 20km south of the Imperial Palace, **Haneda Airport** (ⓦhaneda-airport.jp) is where most domestic flights touch down, as well as a healthy roster of international services. From Haneda, it's a short monorail journey (every 5–10min, 5.20am–11.15pm; 13–19min; ¥490) to Hamamatsuchō station on the JR Yamanote line. Alternatively, you can board a Keihin Kūkō-line train to Shinagawa or Sengakuji and connect directly with other rail and subway lines. A taxi from Haneda to central Tokyo costs ¥4000–8000.

By rail

Shinkansen trains from western Japan pull into **Tokyo station** and **Shinagawa station**, around 6km southwest. Most Shinkansen services from the north also arrive at Tokyo station, via **Ueno station**, some 4km northeast of the Imperial Palace. Tokyo, Shinagawa and Ueno stations are all on the Yamanote line and are connected to several subway lines, putting them within reach of most of the capital. Other long-distance JR services stop at Tokyo and Ueno stations, Shinjuku station on Tokyo's west side and Ikebukuro station in the city's northwest corner.

By bus

Long-distance buses pull in at several major stations around the city, making transport connections straightforward. The main overnight services from Kyoto and Ōsaka arrive at the eastern Yaesu exit of Tokyo station; other buses arrive at Ikebukuro, Shibuya, Shinagawa and Shinjuku.

Getting around

Tokyo's public transport system is efficient, clean and safe, with trains and subways the best way of getting around; a lack of signs in English makes the bus system a lot more challenging. For short, cross-town journeys, taxis are handy and, if shared by a group of people, not all that expensive. Sightseeing tours are also worth considering if you are pushed for time or would like a guided commentary.

By subway

Its colourful map may look daunting, but Tokyo's **subway** is relatively easy to negotiate: the simple colour-coding on trains and maps, as well as clear signposts (many also in English), directional arrows and alpha-numeric station codes, make this by far the most *gaijin*-friendly form of transport. You'll have a much less crowded journey if you avoid travelling at rush hour (7.30–9am & 5–7.30pm).

There are two systems, the nine-line **Tokyo Metro** (ⓦwww.tokyometro. jp) and the four-line **Toei** (ⓦwww. kotsu.metro.tokyo.jp). The systems share some stations, but unless you buy a dual-system ticket, or have a transport pass (see page 121), you cannot switch mid-journey between the two sets of lines. Subways also connect to overland train lines, such as the Yamanote. A colour **map** of the subway system appears at the front of this book.

Tickets (usually ¥170–370) are bought at the vending machines beside the electronic ticket gates; the machines have multi-language functions. Trains run frequently from around 5am to just after midnight; maps close to the ticket barriers, and often on the platforms themselves, indicate where the exits emerge.

For **planning journeys** on both subway and regular trains, the route function on Google Maps (ⓦmaps. google.com) usually works like a charm.

By train

Japan Railways East (ⓦjreast.co.jp) runs the main overland services in and around Tokyo, and there are also several **private railways**, including lines run by Odakyū, Tōbu, Seibu and Tōkyū. They all have their own colour coding on maps, with the various JR lines coming in many different shades – take care not to confuse these with those of the subway network. The famous JR **Yamanote train line** (shown in green on network maps, and indicated by green flashes on the trains) loops around the city centre.

The lowest **fare** on JR lines is ¥140. Ticket machines are easy to operate if buying single tickets, if you can find your destination on the network maps above. Prepaid cards (see page 121) work at the ticket gates.

By monorail

Tokyo has a couple of monorail systems: the **Tokyo monorail**, which runs from Hamamatsuchō to Haneda Airport (see page 120); and the **Yurikamome monorail**, which

Transport passes and travel cards

Both Tokyo Metro and Toei have **24-hour tickets** for use on their respective subway systems (¥600 and ¥700 respectively, or ¥800 covering both systems). JR also has its own one-day pass (¥750). The most convenient way to travel is to use a **Pasmo** (ⓦwww. pasmo.co.jp) or JR **Suica** stored-value card; both can be used on all subways and trains, and most buses, in the wider Tokyo area. The card can be purchased (minimum spend ¥2000, including ¥500 refundable deposit) and recharged at ticket machines in metro and JR stations.

connects Shimbashi with Toyosu via Odaiba. These services operate like the city's private rail lines – you buy separate tickets for journeys on them or travel using the various stored-value cards, such as Pasmo and Suica (see page 121).

By bus

Buses are a good way of cutting across the few areas of Tokyo not served by a subway or train line, though they're little used by overseas visitors. The final destination is listed on the front of the bus, along with the route number. You pay on entry, by dropping the flat rate (¥210) into the fare box by the driver (there's a machine in the box for changing notes); travel cards are also accepted.

By bicycle

You'll see people **cycling** all over Tokyo, but despite this it's not a terribly bike-friendly city. Most locals cycle on the pavement, there being very few dedicated bike lanes, and Japanese rules of courtesy dictate that even though every bike has a bell, absolutely nobody uses them. Docomo's Community Cyle (ⓦdocomo-cycle.jp) is one of the easiest means of getting hold of a bike, with docks across the city; after registering online with your bank card and receiving a pass code, it's ¥150 for the first half-hour, then ¥100 for each subsequent one.

By ferry

The Tokyo Cruise Ship Company (ⓦsuijobus.co.jp) runs several **ferry** services in and around Tokyo Bay; their large picture windows give a completely different view of the city from the one you'll get on the streets. The popular Sumida-gawa service (every 30–50min, 10am–6.30pm; 40min; ¥860) plies the route between **Hinode Pier** on Tokyo Bay and **Asakusa** to the northeast of the city centre. Some boats call at the **Hama Rikyū Teien**, entry to which is often included with the ticket price; you can also head to Hinode from Odaiba (20min; ¥520). For a little more you can travel on the *Himiko* or the *Hotaluna*, near-identical space-age ferries that run from Asakusa to Odaiba (6 daily; ¥1720), sometimes via Hinode.

By taxi

For short hops, **taxis** are often the best option. The basic rate is ¥410 for the first 1km, after which the meter racks up ¥80 every 237m, plus a time charge when the taxi is moving at less than 10km per hour. Between 11pm and 5am, rates are 25 percent higher.

Most taxis have a limit of four passengers. There's never any need to open or close the passenger doors, which are operated by the taxi driver – trying to do it manually can damage the mechanism. It's always a good idea to have the name and address of your destination clearly written on a piece of paper (in Japanese, if possible).

When flagging down a taxi, a red light next to the driver means the cab is free; green means it's occupied. There are designated stands in the busiest parts of town; after the trains stop at night, be prepared for long queues.

Uber (ⓦuber.com) is also functional in Tokyo, though barely any cheaper than the regular cabs (in fact, often more expensive), though there are no late-night surcharges.

Tours

For a quick overview of Tokyo there are the usual **bus tours**, offered by operations such as Hato Bus (ⓦwww.hatobus.com), Japan Grey Line (ⓦwww.jgl.co.jp) and Sky Bus, ranging from half-day jaunts around the central sights (around ¥4500, excluding lunch) to visits out to Kamakura, Nikkō and Hakone.

If bus tours are not your cup of tea, but you still fancy having a guide on hand, you might consider Eyexplore Tokyo for photo-tours (⌨ eyexploretokyo.com), His Go for cultural experiences (⌨ www.hisgo.com), Tokyo Great Cycling Tour for guided bike tours (⌨ tokyocycling.jp), or Street Kart for go-kart tours inspired by Nintendo's Mario Kart game (⌨ kart.st).

Directory A–Z

Addresses

When written in English, Japanese addresses usually follow the Western order of small to big; this is the system we adopt in this guide, with the numbers and district given for each address. For example, the address 2-12-7 Roppongi identifies building number 7, somewhere on block 12 of number 2 **chōme** in Roppongi district. This might be preceded by a building name, and/or the relevant floor number on that building.

Actually locating an address on the ground can be frustrating, even for locals, but thankfully Google Maps searches are usually accurate.

Crime

Tokyo boasts one of the lowest crime rates of any major city in the world; there's little theft, and drug-related crimes are relatively rare. In theory, you should carry your **passport** or ID at all times, but in practice you'll only need it to check into hotels. Carrying **drugs** is a serious no-no; you'll be fined and deported, or sent to prison.

The generally low status of women in Japan is reflected in the amount of **groping** that still goes on in crowded commuter trains. If you do have the misfortune to be groped, the best solution is to grab the offending hand, yank it high in the air and embarrass the person as much as possible.

Fortunately, more violent sexual attacks are rare, though harassment, stalking and rape are seriously underreported. Women should exercise the same caution about being alone with a man as they would anywhere – violent crimes against women are rare, but they do occur. **Tokyo Metropolitan Police** run an English-language hotline (T03 3501 0110; Mon–Fri 8.30am–5.15pm). Another useful option is **Tokyo English Language Lifeline** (TELL; Wesley Center 2F, 6-10-11 Minami-Aoyama, Minato-ku, Tokyo, 107-0062; ☎ 03 5774 0992, ⌨ telljp.com; daily 10am–3pm).

Earthquakes

Japan is home to one-tenth of the world's major earthquakes – at least one quake is recorded every day somewhere in the country, though fortunately the vast majority consist of **minor tremors** that you probably won't even notice. Buildings have been designed to withstand even the most powerful 'quakes, but if you do have the misfortune to experience more than a minor rumble, extinguish any fires and turn off electrical appliances. Open any doors leading out of the room, as they can get jammed shut, blocking your exit. Stay away from windows, to avoid the danger of splintering glass; if you have time, draw the curtains. Don't rush outside (many people are injured by falling masonry), but get under something solid, such as a ground-floor doorway, or a desk. If you are outside when the quake hits, beware of falling objects and head for the nearest park or other open space.

Emergency numbers

Police ☎ 110
Fire or ambulance ☎ 119

Electricity

Mains **electricity** in Tokyo is 100V, 50Hz AC. Japanese plugs have two flat pins or, less commonly, three pins (two flat and one rounded, earth pin). If you are arriving from North America or Canada, the voltage difference should cause no problems with computers, digital cameras, cell phones and the like. Appliances such as hair dryers, curling irons and travel kettles should also work, but not quite as efficiently, in which case you may need a converter. Large hotels can often provide voltage converters and adaptors.

Embassies and consulates

Australia 2-1-14 Mita ☎ 03 5232 4111, ⓦ japan.embassy.gov.au; **Canada** 7-3-38 Akasaka ☎ 03 5412 6200, ⓦ japan.gc.ca; **China** 3-4-33 Moto-Azabu ☎ 03 3403 3064, ⓦ www. china-embassy.or.jp; **Ireland** 2-10-7 Kōjimachi ☎ 03 3263 0695, ⓦ irishembassy.jp; **New Zealand** 20-40 Kamiyamachō ☎ 03 3467 2271, ⓦ nzembassy.com/japan; **South Africa** 4F 1-4 Kojimachi ☎ 03 3265 3366, ⓦ sajapan.org; **UK** 1 Ichibanchō ☎ 03 5211 1100, ⓦ ukinjapan.fco.gov.uk; **USA** 1-10-5 Akasaka ☎ 03 3224 5000, ⓦ jp.usembassy.gov.

Health

To find an English-speaking doctor and the hospital or clinic best suited to your needs, contact the **Tokyo Medical Information Service** (Mon–Fri 9am–8pm; ☎ 03 5285 8181, ⓦ www.himawari.metro.tokyo.jp), who can also provide emergency medical translation over the phone. You should find English-speaking staff at the **American Pharmacy** (Marunouchi Building, 2-4-1 Marunouchi ☎ 03 5220 7716), **St Luke's International Hospital** (9-1 Akashichō ☎ 03 3541 5151, ⓦ hospital.luke.or.jp), and the 24hr **Tokyo Adventist Hospital** (3-17-3 Amanuma ☎ 03 3392 6151).

Internet access

Wi-fi access is finally becoming more widespread in Tokyo. Most big-city **cafés** offer it for free, and it's par for the course at **hostels and hotels**. Wi-fi has now been rolled out in most **subway stations** and **convenience stores** (of which 7-Eleven provides the easiest means of getting online) – you have to register once, with a fake email address if necessary, then log in each time.

Laundry

All hotels provide either a laundry service or coin-operated machines. These typically cost ¥200–300 for a wash (powder ¥30–50) and ¥100–200 for ten minutes in the drier. Neighbourhood laundromats are everywhere.

Left luggage

Most hotels will keep luggage for a few days. The baggage room (daily 7.30am–8.30pm) at Tokyo station can hold bags for the day for ¥600; the station information desks will point the way. Coin lockers can be found in many metro stations (¥400–800, depending on size), but can only be used for a maximum of three days.

LGBTQ travellers

LGBTQ travellers should have few concerns about visiting Tokyo. Japan has no laws against homosexual activity, and outward discrimination is very rare; two people of the same sex sharing a room will hardly raise an eyebrow. General codes of behaviour mean that public displays of affection between any couple, gay or straight, are very rare. There's a decent number of LGBTQ venues, particularly in the Shinjuku Nichōme area (see page 101); you'll find good info online at Fridae (◎fridae.asia), Tokyo Wrestling (◎tokyowrestling.com) and Utopia (◎utopia-asia.com).

Mail

Japan's **mail** service is highly efficient and fast, with thousands of post offices scattered across the capital. All post can be addressed in Western script (*rōmaji*), provided that it's clearly printed. Major post offices that are open 24/7 include the **Central Post Office**, on the west side of Tokyo station.

Money

The **Japanese currency** is the **yen** (*en* in Japanese). Notes are available in denominations of ¥1000, ¥2000 (rarely seen), ¥5000 and ¥10,000, while coins come in values of ¥1, ¥5, ¥10, ¥50, ¥100 and ¥500. Apart from the ¥5 piece, a copper-coloured coin with a hole in the centre, all other notes and coins indicate their value in Western numerals.

Though **credit and debit cards** are far more widely accepted than they were a few years ago, Japan is still very much a cash society. Most convenience stores operate ATMs that accept foreign-issued cards, and you can change cash at the **exchange counters** of main post offices and certain banks.

Tipping is not customary in Japan – take all the change you're given, lest the one giving it to you feels obliged to chase you down the street.

Opening hours and public holidays

Business hours are generally Monday to Friday 9am to 5pm, though private companies often close much later in the evening and may also open on Saturday mornings. Department stores and bigger **shops** tend to open around 10am and shut at 7 or 8pm. Local shops, however, will generally stay open later, while most convenience stores stay open 24 hours. Most shops take one day off a week, not necessarily on a Sunday.

The majority of **museums** close on a Monday, but stay open on Sundays and national holidays; last entry is normally thirty minutes before closing. Most museums and department stores stay open on **national holidays** and take the following day off instead. However, during the New Year festival (January 1–3), Golden Week (April 29–May 5) and O-bon (the week around August 15), almost everything shuts down. Around these periods transport and accommodation can get booked out weeks in advance, and all major tourist spots get overrun.

Phones

You're rarely far from a payphone in Tokyo. The vast majority take both

Consumption tax

A **consumption tax** (*shōhizei*) of 10 percent is levied on virtually all goods and services in Japan, including restaurant meals and accommodation. Tax is supposed to be included in the advertised price, though you'll come across plenty of shops, hotels, restaurants and bars which leave it off.

coins (¥10 and ¥100) and **phone-cards**; they don't give change but do return unused coins, so for local calls use ¥10 rather than ¥100 coins. Everywhere in Japan has an **area code** (Tokyo's is ☎03), which can be omitted if the call is a local one. All toll-free numbers begin with either ☎0120 or ☎0088. Numbers starting with ☎080 or ☎090 belong to mobiles.

Most foreign **models** will work in Japan – contact your mobile phone service provider before leaving your home country. Another solution for short-term visitors is to **rent** a phone at the airport., or track down outlets (usually easiest around major train stations) selling pocket wi-fi "eggs"; plans with a decent amount of data tend to cost ¥750 per day, up to ¥10,000 for a month (check online at ⓦen.wifi-rental-store.jp, or ⓦpupuruwifi.com).

Smoking
Smoking laws in Japan verge on the ridiculous – the practice is banned in public spaces but not inside bars and restaurants, so while you'll see smokers huddled like penguins in dedicated zones on the street, you'll regularly find people lighting up next to you over your meal, coffee or beer. Tighter restrictions have been mooted, but in this conservative land these things take serious time – and, it has to be said, the Japanese are serious smokers.

Time
Tokyo is nine hours ahead of Greenwich Mean Time, fourteen hours ahead of New York, seventeen hours ahead of Los Angeles and two hours behind Sydney. There is no daylight saving time, so during British Summer Time, for example, the difference drops to eight hours.

Tourist information
There are tourist information booths at both airports and all major train stations. If you're in Asakusa, try the **Asakusa Culture and Sightseeing Centre** (2-18-9 Kaminarimon; ☎03 3842 5566); in Ginza head to the **Tokyo City i** (B1F Kitte Building, 2-7-2 Marunouchi; ⓦen.tokyocity-i.jp); and in Shinjuku try the **Tokyo Tourist Information Centre** (1F Tokyo Metropolitan Government No. 1 Building, 2-8-1 Nishi-Shinjuku; ☎03 5321 3077, ⓦgotokyo.org).

Travellers with disabilities
Disability has always been something of an uncomfortable topic in Japan, with disabled people generally hidden from public view. In recent years, however, there has been a certain shift in public opinion; the government is spearheading a drive to provide more accessible hotels and other facilities. All train and subway **stations** now have an extra-wide manned ticket gate and an increasing number have escalators or lifts. Some **trains**, such as the Narita Express, have spaces for wheelchair users, but you should reserve well in advance. Similarly, most modern shopping complexes, museums and other public buildings are equipped with ramps, wide doors and accessible toilets.

While things are improving, Tokyo is not an easy place to get around for anyone using a wheelchair, or for those who find it difficult to negotiate stairs or walk long distances. For further information and help, contact the **Japanese Red Cross Society** (1-1-3 Shiba Daimon, Minato-ku, Tokyo 105-8521). You'll find useful information on their website (ⓦaccessible.jp.org).

Travelling with children
What with Japan being the land of anime, manga and a treasure chest of must-have toys and computer games, you'll have no problem

selling the kids on a trip to Tokyo. It's a safe, child-friendly city that offers a vast number of ways to distract and entertain kids of every age. For families who don't mind bedding down together, a ryokan or Japanese-style room in a hotel, where you can share a big tatami room, is ideal. At most attractions, school-age children get **reduced rates**. Children under 6 ride free on trains, subways and buses, while those aged 6–11 pay half fare. **Nappies**, **baby food** and pretty much anything else you may need are widely available in supermarkets and pharmacies. While **breast-feeding** in public is generally accepted, it's best to be as discreet as possible; most Japanese women who breast-feed use the private rooms provided in department stores and public buildings. Only at the more upmarket Western-style hotels will you be able to arrange **babysitting**; Poppins (ⓦpoppins.co.jp) is one reputable baby-sitting service.

We've listed a selection of amusement and **theme parks** and there's also the wonderful Ghibli Museum in Mitaka (see page 98), Ueno Zoo (see page 46), and child-friendly **museums** such as Ueno's National Science Museum (see page 47), Odaiba's Miraikan (see page 62) and the Edo-Tokyo Museum in Ryōgoku (see page 99). Also check out the listings for **toyshops** and those specializing in manga, anime and character product goods.

Visas

Citizens of Ireland, the UK and certain other European countries can stay in Japan for up to ninety days without a visa provided they are visiting for tourism or business purposes; this stay can be **extended** for another three months. Citizens of Australia, Canada, New Zealand and the US can also stay for up to ninety days without a visa, though this is not extendable and you are required to be in possession of a return air ticket.

Festivals and events

No matter when you visit Tokyo, chances are there'll be a religious festival (*matsuri*) taking place somewhere – fantastic fun for first-time visitors and old Tokyo hands alike. You'll find details of upcoming events online on the official city site (ⓦgotokyo.org). The dates given in the festival listings here can vary according to the lunar calendar, so check ahead if you wish to attend a particular event.

Of the major events listed, by far the most important is **New Year**, when most of the city closes down for a week (roughly Dec 28–Jan 3). Tokyo also hosts three grand **sumo tournaments** each year, as well as film, theatre and music festivals.

Dezomeshiki

January 6. At Tokyo Big Sight in Odaiba, firemen in Edo-period costume pull off dazzling stunts atop long bamboo ladders.

Seijin-no-hi (Coming-of-Age Day)

Second Monday in January. A colourful pageant of 20-year-old women visit city shrines in traditional dress to celebrate their entry into adulthood.

Dezomeshiki (Anime Japan)

Late March. ⓦanime-japan.jp. Three-day event during which Japan's anime industry displays its shows and films for the coming year.

Hanami parties

With the arrival of spring in late March or early April, a pink tide of **cherry blossom** washes north over Tokyo, lasting little more than a week. The finest displays are along the moat around the Imperial Palace (particularly the section close by Yasukuni-jinja), in Ueno-kōen, Aoyama Cemetery, Shinjuku Gyoen, the riverside Sumida-kōen and on the banks of the Meguro-gawa by Nakameguro station, where every tree shelters a blossom-viewing (**hanami**) party.

Art Fair Tokyo

April. Ⓦ artfairtokyo.com. Tokyo International Forum is the focus for Japan's largest commercial art event, with around a hundred local and national galleries participating.

Hana Matsuri

April 8. The Buddha's birthday is celebrated in all Tokyo's temples with either parades or quieter celebrations, during which a small statue of Buddha is sprinkled with sweet tea.

Rainbow Pride

Early May. Ⓦ tokyorainbowpride. com. The largest Pride event in the country, usually featuring a suitably colourful parade.

Roppongi Art Night

Late May. Ⓦ roppongiartnight.com. Dusk-to-dawn street performances and art events are held across Tokyo's party district.

Sanka Matsuri

Third weekend in May. Tokyo's most boisterous festival, when over one hundred *mikoshi* are jostled through the streets of Asakusa, accompanied by lion dancers, geisha and musicians.

Fuji Rock

Late July. The biggest event on the Japanese musical calendar, and a major draw for both bands and festival-goers from overseas.

Lantern Festivals

Late July and early August. Connected to O-bon (see page 125), this tradition sees paper lanterns floated down various waterways, including the Imperial Palace moat.

Hanabi Taikai

Late July and early August. The summer skies explode with thousands of fireworks, harking back to traditional "river-opening" ceremonies. The Sumida-gawa display is the most spectacular.

Summer Sonic

Mid-August. Ⓦ summersonic.com. Two-day rock festival.

Asakusa Samba Carnival

Last Saturday in August. Rio comes to the streets of Asakusa with this spectacular parade of sequinned and feathered dancers – it might sound a bit random, but there are over 200,000 Brazilians living in Japan.

Festival/Tokyo

October to December. Ⓦ www. festival-tokyo.jp. Major theatre and performing arts events, held at various venues across the city.

Tokyo International Film Festival

Late October and early November. Ⓦ tiff-jp.net. Major film festival at which a slew of works from Japan and beyond are shown on screens around the city.

Chronology

628 AD Sensō-ji constructed in Asakusa, after local fishermen find a golden bodhisattva statue in their nets.

1180 First use of Tokyo's original name, Edo, meaning "river gate" – at that point nothing more than a fishing village, it was to become the largest city on earth.

1185 Minamoto clan victorious in Genpei wars; base themselves in Kamakura, just west of Tokyo. Japan settled into a period of semi-feudalism, with peasants allowed tenure of land in return for service to their loyal lord.

1333 The Mongol invasions of the late thirteenth century – thwarted by typhoons, dubbed the kamikaze or "divine wind" by the Japanese of the time – contribute to the fall of the Kamakura government, which in 1333 found itself roundly beaten by the forces of Emperor Go-Daigo.

1457 First castle erected by Ōta Dōkan, now regarded as the founder of modern Tokyo; his battlements formed part of what is now the Higashi Gyoen, which abuts today's Imperial Palace.

1467–77 Ōnin wars effectively relieve the government of authority, and regional *daimyō* (feudal warlords) fight for dominance – a pattern that continued for over a century.

1590 Warlord Tokugawa Ieyasu establishes power base in Edo.

1600 Ieyasu reunites country, and declares himself shogun – effectively a military dictator. Though the emperor continued to hold court in Kyoto, Japan's real centre of power would henceforth lie in Edo, at this point still little more than a small huddle of buildings at the edge of the Hibiya inlet.

1639 Policy of national seclusion introduced; by this time, an estimated 250,000 Japanese Christians had been executed, imprisoned or forced to apostatize.

1640 Completion of Edo Castle, the most imposing in all Japan, and probably the largest in the whole world – a sixteen-kilometre perimeter line of defences complete with a five-storey central keep, a double moat and a complex, spiralling network of canals.

1657 "Fire of the Long Sleeves" lays waste to most of Shitamachi, killing an estimated 100,000 people.

1853 Matthew Perry arrives with the "Black Ships", demanding that Japan open at least some of its ports to foreigners. Japan's ruling elite was thrown into turmoil – it quickly became clear that its military was no longer up to the task.

1858 Japan opens up to foreign trade; treaties were concluded with Western nations, and foreigners given the right of residence and certain judicial rights in these enclaves.

1867 The "Meiji restoration" – shogun Tokugawa Yoshinobu formally applies to the emperor to have imperial power restored, terminating the shogunate, and ushering in a period dubbed Meiji, or "enlightened rule".

1869 Power transferred from Kyoto out west to Edo, which becomes imperial capital; renamed Tokyo ("eastern capital").

1923 The Great Kantō Earthquake strikes at noon on September 1; half of Tokyo – by then a city of some two million – was destroyed, while 100,000 people lost their lives in the quake itself and in the blazes sparked by thousands of cooking-fires.

1942 First US bombs fall on Tokyo in World War II.

1945 World War II ends; Japan falls under American occupation. From a prewar population of nearly seven million, Tokyo was reduced to around three million people in a state of near-starvation.

1964 Hosting of Olympic Games, a hugely successful event which confirmed Tokyo's rise from the wartime ashes, and showed the reborn city off to the world.

1979–81 A technological boom period; in 1979 Sony's Walkman is invented, and in 1981 Mario makes his first appearance in Donkey Kong.

Late 1980s Boom-time in Tokyo: the "bubble years" see land prices in Tokyo reach dizzying heights, matched by excesses of every conceivable sort – everything from gold-wrapped sushi to mink toilet-seat covers.

1992 The economic bubble bursts, with the stock market rapidly sinking and businesses contracting.

1995 Sarin attack on Tokyo subway, leaving twelve dead and thousands injured.

2002 Japan co-hosts FIFA World Cup with South Korea.

2011 Tokyo rattled by the gigantic Tōhoku earthquake, which kills thousands in the north of the country.

2019 Tokyo is the sole host of the Rugby World Cup; the first country in Asia to do so.

2020 Tokyo hosts Olympic Games for the second time.

Language

Picking up a few words of Japanese is not difficult – pronunciation is simple and standard and there are few exceptions to the straightforward grammar rules. With just a little effort you should be able to read the words spelled out in *hiragana* and *katakana*, Japanese phonetic characters, even if you can't understand them. And any time spent learning Japanese will be amply rewarded by delighted locals, who'll always politely comment on your fine linguistic ability. However, it takes a very great effort to master Japanese. The primary stumbling block is the thousands of **kanji** characters (Chinese ideograms) that need to be memorized, all of which

have at least two pronunciations (often many, many more), depending on the sentence and their combination with other characters.

Japanese is written in a combination of three systems. To be able to read a newspaper, you'll need to know around two thousand *kanji*, much more difficult than it sounds, since what each one means varies with its context. The easier writing systems to pick up are the phonetic syllabaries, **hiragana** and **katakana**. Both have 46 regular characters, and can be learned within a couple of weeks. *Hiragana* is used for Japanese words, while *katakana*, with the squarer characters, is used mainly for "loan words" borrowed from other languages (especially English) and technical names. **Rōmaji**, the roman script used to spell out Japanese words, is also used in advertisements and magazines.

Personal pronouns

I Watashi 私
I (familiar, men only) Boku ぼく
You Anata あなた
You (familiar) Kimi きみ
He Kare 彼
She Kanojo 彼女
We Watashi-tachi 私たち
You (plural) Anata-tachi あなたたち
They (male/female) Karera/Kanojo-tachi 彼ら/彼女たち
They (objects) Sorera それら

Basic communications

Yes Hai はい
No Iie/Chigaimasu いいえ/違います
OK Daijōbu/Ōkē 大丈夫/オーケー
Please (offering something) Dōzo どうぞ
Please (asking for something) Onegai shimasu お願いします
Excuse me Sumimasen/Shitsurei shimasu すみません/失礼します
I'm sorry Gomen nasai/Sumimasen ごめんなさい/すみません
Thanks (informal) Dōmo どうも
Thank you Arigatō ありがとう
Thank you very much Dōmo arigatō gozaimasu どうもありがとうございます
What? Nani? なに
When? Itsu? いつ
Where? Doko? どこ
Who? Dare? だれ
This Kore これ
That Sore それ
That (over there) Are あれ
How many? Ikutsu? いくつ
How much? Ikura? いくら
I want (x) (x) ga hoshii desu (x)が欲しいです
I don't want (x) (x) ga irimasen (x)がいりません

Is it possible ...? ... koto ga dekimasu ka ...ことができますか
Is it ...? ... desu ka ...ですか
Can you please help me? Tetsudatte kuremasen ka 手伝ってくれませんか
I can't speak Japanese Nihongo ga hanasemasen 日本語が話せません
I can't read Japanese Nihongo ga yomemasen 日本語が読めません
Can you speak English? Eigo ga dekimasu ka 英語ができますか
Is there someone who can interpret? Tsūyaku wa imasu ka 通訳はいますか
Could you please speak more slowly? Motto yukkuri hanashite kuremasen ka もっとゆっくり話してくれませんか
Could you say that again please? Mō ichido itte kuremasen ka もう一度言ってくれませんか
I understand/I see Wakarimasu/Naruhodo 分かります/なるほど
I don't understand Wakarimasen 分かりません
What does this mean? Kore wa dōiu imi desu ka これはどういう意味ですか
How do you say (x) in Japanese? Nihongo de (x) o nan-te iimasu ka 日本語で(x)を何て言いますか
What's this called? Kore wa nan-to iimasu ka これは何と言いますか
How do you pronounce this character? Kono kanji wa nan-te yomimasu ka この漢字は何て読みますか
Please write in English/Japanese Eigo/Nihongo de kaite kudasai 英語/日本語で書いてください

Greetings and basic courtesies

Hello/Good day Konnichiwa 今日は
Good morning Ohayō gozaimasu おはようございます
Good evening Konbanwa 今晩は
Good night (when leaving) Osaki ni お先に
Good night (when going to bed) Oyasuminasai お休みなさい
How are you? O-genki desu ka お元気ですか
I'm fine Genki desu 元気です

I'm fine, thanks Okagesama de
おかげさまで

How do you do/Nice to meet you
Hajimemashite はじめまして

Don't mention it/you're welcome Dō
itashimashite どういたしまして

I'm sorry Gomen nasai ごめんなさい

Just a minute please Chotto matte kudasai
ちょっと待ってください

What's your name? Shitsurei desu ga
o-namae wa 失礼ですがお名前は

My name is (x) Namae wa (x) desu
名前は(x)です

Goodbye Sayonara/Sayōnara
さよなら/さようなら

Goodbye (informal) Dewa mata/Jā ne
では又/じゃあね

Chitchat

Where are you from? O-kuni wa doko desu
ka お国はどこですか

Britain Eikoku/Igirisu 英国/イギリス

Ireland Airurando アイルランド

America Amerika アメリカ

Australia Ōsutoraria オーストラリア

Canada Kanada カナダ

New Zealand Nyū Jiirando
ニュージーランド

Japan Nihon 日本

How old are you? O-ikutsu desu ka
おいくつですか

I am (x) years old (x) sai desu (x)
際です

Are you married? Kekkon shite imasu ka
結婚していますか

I am married/not married Kekkon shite
imasu/imasen
結婚しています/いません

Do you like ...? ... suki desu ka
好きですか

I like ... suki desu ...好きです

I don't like ... suki dewa arimasen
...好きではありません

What's your job? O-shigoto wa nan desu ka
お仕事は何ですか

I work for a company Kaishain desu
会社員です

I'm a tourist Kankō kyaku desu
観光客です

Really? (informal) Hontō 本当

It can't be helped (informal) Shikata ga nai
(formal)/Shō ga nai (informal)
仕方がない/しょうがない

Numbers, time and dates

There are special ways of **counting** different
things in Japanese. The most common first
translation is used when counting time and
quantities and measurements, with added
qualifiers such as minutes (*pun/fun*) or yen
(*en*). The second translations are sometimes
used for counting objects. From ten, there is
only one set of numbers. For four, seven and
nine, alternatives to the first translation are
used in some circumstances.

Zero Zero/rei 0/零

One Ichi 一 Hitotsu ひとつ

Two Ni 二 Futatsu ふたつ

Three San 三 Mittsu みっつ

Four Yon/Shi 四 Yottsu よっつ

Five Go 五 Itsutsu いつつ

Six Roku 六 Muttsu むっつ

Seven Shichi/Nana 七 Nanatsu ななつ

Eight Hachi 八 Yattsu やっつ

Nine Kyū 九 Kokonotsu ここのつ

Ten Jū 十 Tō とう

Eleven Jū-ichi 十一

Twelve Jū-ni 十二

Twenty Ni-jū 二十

Twenty-one Ni-jū-ichi 二十一

Thirty San-jū 三十

One hundred Hyaku 百

Two hundred Ni-hyaku 二百

Thousand Sen 千

Ten thousand Ichi-man 一万

One hundred thousand Jū-man 十万

One million Hyaku-man 百万

One hundred million Ichi-oku 一億

Time and dates

Now Ima 今

Today Kyō 今日

Morning Asa 朝

Evening Yūgata 夕方

Night Yoru/Ban 夜/晩

Tomorrow Ashita 明日

The day after tomorrow Asatte あさって

Yesterday Kinō 昨日

Week Shū 週

Month Getsu/Gatsu 月

Year Nen/Toshi 年
Monday Getsuyōbi 月曜日
Tuesday Kayōbi 火曜日
Wednesday Suiyōbi 水曜日
Thursday Mokuyōbi 木曜日
Friday Kin'yōbi 金曜日
Saturday Doyōbi 土曜日
Sunday Nichiyōbi 日曜日
What time is it? Ima nan-ji desu ka
今何時ですか
It's 10 o'clock Jū-ji desu 十時です
10.20 Jū-ji ni-juppun 十時二十分
10.30 Jū-ji han 十時半
10.50 Jū-ichi-ji juppun mae
十一時十分前
AM Gozen 午前
PM Gogo 午後

Getting around

Aeroplane Hikōki 飛行機
Airport Kūkō 空港
Bus Basu バス
Bus stop Basu tei バス停
Train Densha 電車
Station Eki 駅
Subway Chikatetsu 地下鉄
Ferry Ferii フェリー
Left-luggage office Ichiji azukarijo
一時預かり所
Coin locker Koin rokkā
コインロッカー
Ticket Kippu 切符
Ticket office Kippu uriba 切符売り場
One-way Kata-michi 片道
Return Ōfuku 往復
Bicycle Jitensha 自転車
Taxi Takushii タクシー
Map Chizu 地図
Straight ahead Massugu まっすぐ
In front of Mae 前
Right Migi 右
Left Hidari 左
North Kita 北
South Minami 南
East Higashi 東
West Nishi 西

Places

Temple Otera/Odera/-ji/-in
お寺/-寺/-院

Shrine Jinja/Jingū/-gū/-taisha
神社/神宮/-宮/-大社
Castle -jō 城
Park Kōen 公園
River Kawa/Gawa 川
Street Tōri/Dōri/Michi 通り/道
Bridge Hashi/Bashi 橋
Museum Hakubutsukan 博物館
Art gallery Bijutsukan 美術館
Garden Niwa/Teien/-en 庭/庭園/-園
Island Shima/-jima/-tō 島/-島
Hill Oka 丘
Mountain Yama/-san/-take 山/-山/-岳
Hot spring spa Onsen 温泉
Lake Mizu-umi/-ko 湖/-湖

Accommodation

Hotel Hoteru ホテル
Traditional-style inn Ryokan 旅館
Guesthouse Minshuku 民宿
Youth hostel Yūsu hosuteru ユースホステル
Single room Shinguru rūmu
シングルルーム
Double room Daburu rūmu ダブルルーム
Twin room Tsuin rūmu ツインルーム
Dormitory Kyōdō/Ōbeya 共同/大部屋
Japanese-style room Washitsu 和室
Western-style room Yōshitsu 洋室
Western-style bed Beddo ベッド
Bath O-furo お風呂
Do you have any vacancies? Kūshitsu wa
arimasu ka 空室はありますか
I'd like to make a reservation Yoyaku o shitai
no desu ga 予約をしたいのですが
I have a reservation Yoyaku shimashita
予約しました
I don't have a reservation Yoyaku shimasen
deshita 予約しませんでした
How much is it per person? Hitori ikura
desu ka 一人いくらですか
Does that include meals? Shokuji wa tsuite
imasu ka 食事はついていますか
I would like to stay one night/two nights
Hitoban/Futaban tomaritai no desu ga
一晩/二晩泊まりたいのですが
I would like to see the room Heya o misete
kudasaimasen ka
部屋を見せてくださいませんか
Key Kagi 鍵
Passport Pasupōto パスポート

Shopping, money and banks

Shop Mise 店
How much is it? Kore wa ikura desu ka
これはいくらですか
It's too expensive Taka-sugimasu
高すぎます
Is there anything cheaper? Mō sukoshi
yasui mono wa arimasu ka
もう少し安いものはありますか
Do you accept credit cards? Kurejitto kādo
wa tsukaemasu ka
クレジットカードは使えますか
I'm just looking Miru dake desu
見るだけです
Foreign exchange Gaikoku-kawase
外国為替
Bank Ginkō 銀行
Travellers' cheque Toraberāzu chekku
トラベラーズチェック
Where is the nearest ATM? Ichiban chikai
ATM wa doko desu ka
一番近いATMはどこですか

Health

Hospital Byōin 病院
Pharmacy Yakkyoku 薬局
Medicine Kusuri 薬
Doctor Isha 医者
Dentist Haisha 歯医者
I'm ill Byōki desu 病気です

Food and drink Basics

Bar Nomiya 飲み屋
Standing-only bar Tachinomiya
立ちのみ屋
Café/coffee shop Kissaten 喫茶店
Cafeteria Shokudō 食堂
Pub Pabu パブ
Pub-style restaurant Izakaya 居酒屋
Restaurant Resutoran レストラン
**Restaurant specializing in charcoal-grilled
foods** Robatayaki 炉端焼
Breakfast Asa-gohan 朝ご飯
Lunch Hiru-gohan 昼ご飯
Dinner Ban-gohan 晩ご飯
Boxed meal Bentō 弁当
Set meal Teishoku 定食
Daily special set meal Higawari-teishoku
日替り定食
Menu Menyū メニュー

Do you have an English menu? Eigo no
menyū wa arimasu ka
英語のメニューはありますか
How much is that? Ikura desu ka
いくらですか
I would like (a) ... (a)... o onegai shimasu
(a)をお願いします
May I have the bill? Okanjō o onegai shimasu
お勘定をお願いします
I am a vegetarian Watashi wa bejitarian desu
私はベジタリアンです
Can I have it without meat? Niku nashi de
onegai dekimasu ka
肉なしでお願いできますか

Staple foods

Bean curd tofu Tōfu 豆腐
Bread Pan パン
Butter Batā バター
Dried seaweed Nori のり
Egg Tamago 卵
Fermented soyabean paste Miso 味噌
Garlic Ninniku にんにく
Oil Abura 油
Pepper Koshō こしょう
Rice Gohan ご飯
Salt Shio 塩
Soy sauce Shōyu しょうゆ
Sugar Satō 砂糖

Fruits and vegetables

Fruit Kudamono 果物
Apple Ringo りんご
Banana Banana バナナ
Grapefruit Gurēpufurūtsu
グレープフルーツ
Grapes Budō ぶどう
Japanese plum Ume うめ
Lemon Remon レモン
Melon Meron メロン
Orange Orenji オレンジ
Peach Momo 桃
Pear Nashi なし
Persimmon Kaki 柿
Pineapple Painappuru パイナップル
Strawberry Ichigo いちご
Tangerine Mikan みかん
Watermelon Suika すいか
Vegetables Yasai 野菜
Salad Sarada サラダ

Aubergine Nasu なす
Beans Mame 豆
Beansprouts Moyashi もやし
Carrot Ninjin にんじん
Cauliflower Karifurawā カリフラワー
Green pepper Piiman ピーマン
Green horseradish Wasabi わさび
Leek Negi ねぎ
Mushroom Kinoko きのこ
Onion Tamanegi たまねぎ
Potato Poteto/Jagaimo
ポテト/じゃがいも
Radish Daikon だいこん
Sweetcorn Kōn コーン
Tomato Tomato トマト

Fish and seafood dishes

Fish Sakana 魚
Shellfish Kai 貝
Raw fish Sashimi さしみ
Sushi Sushi 寿司
Serving of sushi rice with topping Nigiri-
zushi にぎり寿司
Sushi rolled in crisp seaweed Maki-zushi
まき寿司
Bowl of sushi rice topped with fish, egg
and vegetables Chirashi-zushi ちらし寿司
Abalone Awabi あわび
Blowfish Fugu ふぐ
Cod Tara たら
Crab Kani かに
Eel Unagi うなぎ
Herring Nishin にしん
Horse mackerel Aji あじ
Lobster Ise-ebi 伊勢海老
Octopus Tako たこ
Oyster Kaki かき
Prawn Ebi えび
Sea bream Tai たい
Sea urchin Uni うに
Squid Ika いか
Tuna Maguro まぐろ
Yellowtail Buri ぶり

Meat and meat dishes

Meat Niku 肉
Beef Gyūniku 牛肉
Chicken Toriniku 鶏肉
Lamb Ramu ラム
Pork Butaniku 豚肉

Breaded, deep-fried slice of pork Tonkatsu
とんかつ
Chicken, other meat and vegetables
grilled on skewers Yakitori 焼き鳥
Skewers of food dipped in breadcrumbs
and deep-fried Kushiage 串揚げ
Stew including meat (or seafood),
vegetables and noodles Nabe 鍋
Thin beef slices cooked in broth Shabu-
shabu しゃぶしゃぶ
Thin beef slices braised in a sauce Sukiyaki
すきやき

Other dishes

Buddhist-style vegetarian cuisine Shōjin-
ryōri 精進料理
Chinese-style noodles Rāmen ラーメン
Chinese-style dumplings Gyōza ぎょうざ
Fried noodles Yakisoba/Yakiudon
焼そば/焼きうどん
Stewed chunks of vegetables and fish on
skewers Oden おでん
Thin buckwheat noodles Soba そば
Soba in a hot soup Kake-soba かけそば
Cold soba served with a dipping sauce
Zaru-soba/Mori-soba ざるそば/もりそば
Thick wheat noodles Udon うどん
Fried rice Chāhan チャーハン
Lightly battered seafood and vegetables
Tempura 天ぷら
Meat, vegetable and fish cooked in soy
sauce and sweet sake Teriyaki 照り焼き
Mild curry served with rice Karē raisu
カレーライス
Octopus in balls of batter Takoyaki
たこやき
Pounded rice cakes Mochi もち
Rice topped with fish, meat or vegetables
Donburi どんぶり
Rice triangles wrapped in crisp seaweed
Onigiri おにぎり
Savoury pancakes Okonomiyaki
お好み焼き
Japanese-style food Washoku 和食
Japanese haute cuisine Kaiseki-ryōri
懐石料理

Drinks

Beer Biiru ビール
Black tea Kōcha 紅茶

Coffee Kōhii コーヒー
Distilled liquor Shōchū 焼酎
Fruit juice Jūsu ジュース
Green tea Sencha 煎茶
Milk Miruku/Gyūnyū ミルク/牛乳
Oolong tea Ūron-cha ウーロン茶
Powdered green tea Matcha 抹茶

Sake (rice wine) Sake/Nihon-shu
酒/日本酒
Water Mizu 水
Whisky Uisukii ウイスキー
Whisky and water Mizu-wari
水割り
Wine Wain ワイン

Glossary

anime Animated movies or TV shows.

basho Sumo tournament.

bentō Food boxes.

–chō or **machi** Subdivision of the city, smaller than a -ku.

–chōme Area of the city consisting of a few blocks.

daimyō Feudal lords.

–dōri Main road.

Edo Pre-1868 name for Tokyo.

furo Traditional Japanese bath.

futon Bedding.

–gawa/kawa River.

gaijin/gaikokujin Foreigner.

geisha Traditional female entertainer accomplished in the arts.

geta Wooden sandals.

hanami Cherry-blossom viewing.

izakaya Traditional bar, also serving food.

JR Japan Railways.

kabuki Traditional theatre.

kaiseki Japanese haute cuisine.

kaiten-zushi Conveyor-belt sushi restaurant.

kanji Japanese script derived from Chinese characters.

katakana Phonetic script used mainly for writing foreign words in Japanese.

kimono Literally "clothes" but usually referring to women's traditional dress.

kissaten Traditional, independent café.

kōban Local police box.

–kōen Park.

–ku Principal administrative division of the city, usually translated as "ward".

maid café A café where the waitresses are dressed in costumes and role play.

manga Comics.

matsuri Festival.

mikoshi Portable shrine used in festivals.

minshuku Family-run lodge, similar to a bed and breakfast, cheaper than a ryokan.

nō Traditional theatre.

onsen Hot spring, generally developed for bathing.

otaku Obsessive fan mainly of manga and anime but can refer to other things, too.

pachinko Vertical pinball machines.

rotemburo Outdoor hot-spring bath.

ryokan Traditional Japanese inn.

sakura Cherry blossom.

samurai Warrior class who were retainers of the *daimyō*.

sentō Neighbourhood public bath.

shamisen Type of lute.

Shinkansen Bullet train.

Shinto Japan's indigenous animist religion.

Shitamachi Old working-class districts of east Tokyo.

shogun The military rulers of Japan before 1868.

sumo Japan's national sport, a form of heavyweight wrestling which evolved from ancient Shinto divination rites.

tatami Rice-straw matting, the traditional covering for floors.

torii Gate to a Shinto shrine.

yakuza Professional criminal gangs.

yokochō Market-style area, often focusing on food shacks.

yukata Loose cotton dressing gown.

Publishing Information
First edition 2020

Distribution
UK, Ireland and Europe
Apa Publications (UK) Ltd; sales@roughguides.com
United States and Canada
Ingram Publisher Services; ips@ingramcontent.com
Australia and New Zealand
Woodslane; info@woodslane.com.au
Southeast Asia
Apa Publications (SN) Pte; sales@roughguides.com
Worldwide
Apa Publications (UK) Ltd; sales@roughguides.com
Special Sales, Content Licensing and CoPublishing
Rough Guides can be purchased in bulk quantities at discounted prices. We can create special editions, personalised jackets and corporate imprints tailored to your needs. sales@roughguides.com.
roughguides.com
Printed in China by RR Donnelley

All rights reserved
© 2020 Apa Digital (CH) AG
License edition © Apa Publications Ltd UK
No part of this publication may be reproduced, stored in or introduced into a retrieval system, or transmitted in any form, or by any means (electronic, mechanical, photocopying, recording or otherwise) without the prior written permission of the copyright owner.
A catalogue record for this book is available from the British Library

The publishers and authors have done their best to ensure the accuracy and currency of all the information in **Pocket Rough Guide Tokyo**, however, they can accept no responsibility for any loss, injury, or inconvenience sustained by any traveller as a result of information or advice contained in the guide.

Rough Guide Credits
Editor: Aimee White
Cartography: Ed Wright
Managing editor: Rachel Lawrence
Picture editor: Aude Vauconsant
Cover photo research: Sławomir Krajewski

Original design: Richard Czapnik
Senior DTP coordinator: Dan May
Head of DTP and Pre-Press: Rebeka Davies
Layout: Ruth Bradley

Author: Martin Zatko has been in a state of almost continuous motion since 2002, wending his way through 140-odd countries to date, and writing or contributing to almost fifty Rough Guides, including various editions of Japan, Korea, China, Taiwan, Vietnam, Myanmar, India, Turkey, Greece, Morocco and Fiji. Japan keeps drawing him back, and he one day hopes to hitch-hike across the whole country (again).

Acknowledgements

Martin Zatko would like to thank all those who assisted him during his trip around Japan (or were simply able to hang out and be great), including Keisuke Yamamoto and the Freshroom team, super-cool Swiss housemates Miri and Milos, Takako and the team at the Tokyo Convention & Visitors Bureau, Ched for the part-time gig as a whisky and sashimi delivery driver, Soyeon for the trip down memory lane in ever-convenient Nakameguro, the kombini dotted around Senkawa for providing alcohol and snacks around the clock, and various seas and oceans for providing all the fish.

Reader's updates

Thanks to all the readers who have taken the time to write in with comments and suggestions (and apologies if we've inadvertently omitted or misspelt anyone's name): Eva Gunnarsson, Gary Foggo

Help us update

We've gone to a lot of effort to ensure that this edition of the **Pocket Rough Guide Tokyo** is accurate and up-to-date. However, things change – places get "discovered", opening hours are notoriously fickle, restaurants and rooms raise prices or lower standards. If you feel we've got it wrong or left something out, we'd like to know, and if you can remember the address, the price, the hours, the phone number, so much the better.

Please send your comments with the subject line "**Pocket Rough Guide Tokyo Update**" to mail@uk.roughguides.com. We'll credit all contributions and send a copy of the next edition (or any other Rough Guide if you prefer) for the very best emails.

Photo Credits

(Key: T-top; C-centre; B-bottom; L-left; R-right)

300 Bar 38
Alamy 2BR, 15T, 18B, 30, 31, 37, 39, 40, 44, 45, 59, 65, 70, 71, 76, 99, 102
Getty Images 1, 2BL, 6, 12/13T, 49, 50, 78, 90, 101, 108, 110/111, 118/119
H.P.FRANCE S.A 85
iStock 5, 12B, 12/13B, 14T, 15B, 17B, 18T, 18C, 19C, 20T, 20C, 20B, 21T, 21B, 22/23, 24, 27, 29, 32, 35, 36, 43, 51, 54, 68, 93, 105, 107, 109
JNTO 16T, 19B

Martin Richardson/Rough Guides 10, 63
Saori K/JNTO 11B
Shutterstock 2T, 2CR, 13C, 14B, 16B, 17T, 28, 33, 52, 53, 56, 57, 73, 83, 86, 89, 96, 97
Yasufimi Nishi/JNTO 4, 11T, 19T, 21C, 41, 47

Cover: Sensō-ji **Shutterstock**

Index

INDEX

NOTES